From starting a feminist revolution in her hometown of Yakima, WA, to breaking in as a member of the first generation of tradeswomen on construction jobsites in San Francisco, Molly Martin shares a unique and rare view into the the battles, the losses, and the the sweet glory of hard-fought wins of one whose life has been dedicated to claiming space and carving out fairness and equity for women.

Tradeswomen today have Molly and sister tradeswomen of that first generation to thank for what has become a safer space for women to work hard at a job they love and earn a wage that enables a solid middle-class life. They broke down the doors so that we could stride through behind them in our Carhartts and toolbelts; with our union cards, and our business cards; as journey-level workers and as "crew chiefs"; as union leaders and union staff; and, as those in positions of power to make positive changes for tradeswomen and the entire construction industry.

—Sabrina Hernandez, Business Representative
International Brotherhood of Electrical Workers, Local 6, San Francisco

There's no denying Molly Martin is a great storyteller! Molly has always had the uncanny ability to bring humor to her stories, even with subjects difficult to digest. And it is her shoulders that I stand on! As one of the first in our electrical union in San Francisco, she showed me that it was possible!

—Chantel Lewis, San Francisco Electrical Inspector,
IBEW Local 6

For those who lived through these decades, this book will spark a conversation. For those who didn't, Martin's book provides a lively passport to the world of a pioneering tradeswoman and activist who helped to shape her times. Thrilling!

— Jane LaTour, author
<small>Sisters in the Brotherhoods:
Working Women Organizing for Equality in New York City</small>

We are lucky to have had Molly Martin living through the past few momentous decades. Here she collects her inciting and insightful writings. Let's hope her historic contributions are discovered and rediscovered by the coming generations of women (and men) at work, and in the world at large.

—Chris Carlsson, co-director Shaping San Francisco, author <small>Hidden San Francisco: A Guide to Lost Landscapes, Unsung Heroes, and Radical Histories.</small>

Wonder Woman Electric to the Rescue

to the Rescue

A Collection of Memoir, Essays and Short Stories

by Molly Martin

ISBN 9798755103541

Design and layout by Chris Carlsson

Cover photo clockwise from top left: Susanne Di Vincenzo, Molly Martin, Sylvia Israel, Jean Ulbricht, Pat Manns, Val Ramirez. Not pictured: Canyon Sam and Lyn Shimizu.

Van art by Jeanne Clark. On the other side she painted a Black Wonder Woman

Most of these pieces have been previously published in *Tradeswomen, Feminary, Sinister Wisdom, The Stansbury Forum, Foundsf. org, MUNI Diaries, Medium,* and the book *If I Had a Hammer: Women's Work in Poetry, Fiction, and Photographs.*

Tradeswoman Books
970 Hyland Dr.
Santa Rosa, CA 95404

tradeswomn@gmail.com
molly-martin.com

Table of Contents

Introducton 7

MY LIFE IN PARTS
Queer Fashion Bombs a Straight Wedding 13
Women's Equality Day 1970 22
The Last Survivor 28
Single Life 33
How the Lesbians Invaded Bernal Heights 41
Still Standing 47
Gay Man Stabbed in Heart Survives 52
Nuns Take the Castro 57

UNDER CONSTRUCTION
Wonder Woman Electric to the Rescue 63
Machisma on Hayes Street 67
Dispatched 73
Sisters Restoring Justice 77
A Sister Raped and Murdered 82
Workboots Step Out of the Closet 89
How Do You Say Goodbye? 96
Why Would You Want to be a Woman? 101
Call Her by Her Name 106
What Old Tradeswomen Talk About 113

JUST THE FACTS FOREMA'AM
Why I Hate Firemen 117
Fighting for Gender Neutral Language 125
What I know About Stereotyping 130
Men Making Men Look Bad 135
How to Avoid Reproduction 140
Making America White Again 150

TRADESWOMEN FICTION: STORIES OF WORKING WHILE FEMALE
Sweetheart 160
Bathroom Conversation 168
Graffiti War 173
Deck Job 179
Mean Business 184
A Paycheck Away 192
Burros Bonding 197

Introduction

When her father lost his teaching job at the nadir of the Great Depression, my mother, the oldest of four daughters, went to work as a stenographer to support her family, putting her typing and shorthand skills to good use. In her day women were restricted to the lowest paid jobs and in many states married women were not even allowed to work for wages. My mother may have remained single until her mid-thirties because she felt responsible for supporting the family after her father died. She was a proud "career girl."

My mother insisted I take typing and shorthand classes in high school, skills that had allowed her to make a living *working while female*. Mom made it clear to me that if I hoped for any sort of economic independence, I needed marketable skills and I needed to look ahead and see myself as a worker.

It's not surprising that as a young feminist I seized on the issue of work. For me it was the foundation of feminism. To gain independence from men, women needed to be able to make a living wage. And so I became an electrician. Breaking down the barriers to women in the construction trades became my life's work.

My generation of tradeswomen was the second wave of women to enter the trades, after our foremothers who served during wars and were forced to return to unpaid work on the home front at the wars' end. Those women proved *we can do it.* Then, starting in the 1970s, we had to prove it all over again. We asked *why can't I?*

Along with other nontraditional female workers, I founded organizations like Tradeswomen Inc. and San Francisco Women in Trades to advocate for our cause. We had support from allies at the Women's Bureau US Dept. of Labor and Equal Rights Advocates.

In 1981 we started a quarterly magazine, *Tradeswomen* and it became our method of communicating with sisters around the country and the world during the 1980s and 90s.

We wrote about our work lives because we wanted to put this new world we were experiencing into words—the joys of learning new skills and building something with our hands, of creating a sisterhood with other tradeswomen, the trials of responding to sexism and discrimination. We wanted to let readers know what it was like in the world of construction and in other nontraditional jobs, and to let our sister tradeswomen know they were not alone. We wanted to tell the world we had broken barriers and we weren't backing down.

In the process of managing the magazine I interacted with tradeswomen across the country and in 1988 I edited a book of their essays and interviews. *Hard-Hatted Women: Stories of Struggle and Success in the Trades* (Seal Press) anthologizes 26 first person stories of women working in nontraditional jobs. On a low-budget book tour I drove my Honda CRX across the country meeting with groups of tradeswomen in cities along my route.

Networking is key to our organizing. Tradeswomen started convening even before we had jobs, to strategize how to help each other break into the world of "men's work." Tradeswomen Inc. sponsored the first national conference for tradeswomen in 1983. Finally, we were not isolated. We were surrounded by hundreds of women just like us whose main issues were getting work in nontraditional jobs and dealing with harassment once we got there. Then we partnered with the California State Building Trades Council to sponsor annual conferences until they became a national event now sponsored by the National Building Trades Unions. It's the biggest all-craft gathering of tradeswomen in the universe with over 2,000 tradeswomen attending. I was involved in the conferences from their beginning and continue to facilitate workshops on tradeswomen history and the tradeswomen writers workshop. We still need to tell our stories.

I first conceived of this book as a collection of my stories published in *Tradeswomen*. In the magazine I wrote about affirmative action, court cases that affected the laws that protected us, racism and sexism in construction, sexual harassment, and the history of women in nontraditional work. And I interviewed scores of tradeswomen about their work and struggles. I wrote lots of stories for *Tradeswomen*, but the ones that have held up best are fiction, based on my own experience working in the trades. They are included in this book as well as some stories more recently written on the subject. I've also included some of my favorite essays and memoirs that relate to the rest of my life. This is where I come from and how I became an activist.

The first section, *My Life in Parts*, contains memoirs--stories about my family and my life in San Francisco. I tell how my mother and I became feminist activists together, how I came out to my father, how my gender nonconforming brother and I upset the status quo, about gay and lesbian culture in San Francisco during the AIDS years, and the lesbian survivor of the last massacre of Native Americans.

In the second section, *Under Construction*, are memoirs specifically about tradeswomen and my experience in construction. It includes stories about Wonder Woman Electric, an all-female contracting company based in San Francisco, and stories about my time working as a construction electrician and as a maintenance electrician for the City of San Francisco.

The third section, *Just the Facts Forema'm*, is composed of essays, many of which are about nontraditional work and affirmative action. It also includes stories about racism in my hometown and my efforts to take control of my own reproductive life.

The fourth section, *Tradeswomen Fiction: Stories of Working While Female*, contains fiction based on my own experience working construction. All except one of them were published in *Tradeswomen* magazine. I write about forming alliances with men of color and other outcasts, the perils of small contracting, working with other women, and overcoming harassment and discrimination.

We tradeswomen created a movement agitating for high-paid jobs in the construction trades and it's still going strong. We see ourselves as part of the feminist and civil rights movements, making and depending on allies among people of color and women's organizations. We are on the front lines of the movement for women's equity; every day we show up at work on the construction site is revolutionary. We confront some of the worst harassment and discrimination on these jobs, and over the past half century we've collaborated with unions and employers to improve working conditions. I'm so proud to be part of a multi-racial movement which has truly improved the lives and earning power of working class women.

Today in 2021, women are more accepted in the trades than when I first started as an electrician in the 1970s, but they still face isolation and harassment at work. Women are still less than four percent of skilled trades workers. Today tradeswomen interact and gain support through social media. Technology has changed the way we work and the way we communicate, but our struggles continue and the stories of our history remain relevant.

As my hero sister Addie Wyatt, vice president of the Amalgamated Meat Cutters Union, said, "If you don't know where you come from, you don't know where you're going." In this collection you'll have a window on my journey to becoming an activist and you'll see work on the construction site from women's point of view.

MY LIFE IN PARTS

When I was a girl my mother said to me
When you're grown what do you want to be?
For choices I had only three:
Teacher, nurse and secretary.
>   *I wanna join the brotherhood*
>   *Where I can build something and the pay is good*
>   *I'll have a trade and I'll have it made*

—From my song *Sister in the Brotherhood*

Queer Fashion Bombs a Straight Wedding

"Jesus Christ, it's 1979. Why do they need to get married? They've been living together for five years. No one in the family disapproves. Why do people feel compelled to have the state sanction their relationships?"

Don let me rave. Neither of us could answer these rhetorical questions. He couldn't have been any less enthusiastic about our brother Tim's wedding than I was. We knew that neither of us would ever have a family wedding with all the attendant fussing, well-wishing, presents and cultural sanction, not that either of us would want one.

"You don't suppose there's any way we can get out of going," he said in a resigned tone.

I considered this. Our attendance seemed like a small price to pay to avoid the disapprobation that surely would result from our absence. "We can stay in the background. At least we're not being asked to be bridesmaids."

I could hear my brother sigh on the other end of the phone. "To be a bridesmaid," he said, "has always been a great fantasy of mine."

"I see what you mean. If I could be best man, I could rent a tuxedo. Fuck! What will I wear?" Don was silent, and I knew he wasn't worrying about what I'd be wearing.

"Don, if you're thinking about wearing a dress, just forget it right now. This is not the big city or some trendy college community. This is cowboy country. You'll get the shit kicked out of you."

When we said goodbye, I wasn't entirely sure I'd convinced him, and I wondered how my outrageous brother managed to stay alive without me as his constant bodyguard. He insistently challenged assumptions about dress and gender, which was a dangerous thing at a time when the moral majority felt its grasp on the reins of cultural definitions slipping.

The truth was, just by being my natural self, people—both children and adults—were always confronting me about the nature of my gender. They would yell out of windows or from cars as I walked by, "Are you a boy or a girl?" Or I would be mistaken for a gay man. "Faggot!" they would yell, and speed off before I could correct them: "You idiot! I'm a dyke!"

I had learned that knowledge of gender is extremely important to people. They need this information before they know anything else about you. And once they get you pegged, to be surprised can make them inexplicably angry. All their presuppositions are suddenly being challenged. It's like you've called into question some intensely personal assumptions about who *they* are in the world. I figured the problem wasn't me, but how people expected women to look and act. To be feminine required performing unnatural acts—shaving one's body hair, wearing sticky make-up and carefully coiffed hair, being quiet, wearing odd clothes and uncomfortable shoes, walking with short picky strides. I had practiced these ritual gestures at one time, but the feminist movement had released me. I was free and I was never going back now.

Unfortunately, my freedom from convention left me completely unprepared to dress for Tim's wedding. I had no dress-up clothes. As a matter of principle I'd stopped wearing dresses in 1970. Since then the contents of my closet had been recycled from thrift stores. As a working electrician in those days of butch dykedom, I could just wash my flannel shirts and jeans and wear them to the bar.

No one I knew ever got dressed up, and if they attended weddings, they never told me. So what does a nonconforming, revolutionary lesbian wear to a heterosexual wedding?

At the airport I searched the Nordic crowd of Seattleites for Don's dark head. I never knew what to expect. He'd been a hippie with a thick ponytail and full beard last time I'd seen him, but personas changed from year to year. He was not at the gate and I wandered until I heard my name called from a waiting area. Then I saw him, relaxing back into one of the lounge chairs like a queen, newly clean-shaven and wearing giant turquoise butterfly earrings, a flowing scarf wrapped around his shoulder-length hair, tied in back. "I thought it was time to relinquish my male privilege," he smiled.

In the short 150 miles or so between Don's home at the foot of the Olympic Peninsula to our hometown of Yakima, the land cracks and dries up like the edges of those Sisterhood Is Powerful posters you rehang in each new collective house. Snoqualmie Pass takes you from a rich, dripping evergreen rainforest over the snow-capped Cascade Mountains, past ski resorts and the shorn heads of clear-cut hills down into the Kittitas Valley's flat pastures dotted with Black Angus cattle.

Up over the Manastash Ridge, a new freeway replaced the winding two-lane road along the Yakima River. Beyond irrigation, only sagebrush flourishes. From the west side of the ridge you can see the town of Ellensburg surrounded by a patchwork of pastures, ground crops and brown earth, and above that the sharp white peaks of the Wenatchee Range. As you continue east, your nose dries up and your hair electrifies, the sky turns intense blue and if there are clouds they look like puffs of bleached cotton. Then, just before the Yakima Valley appears below, if you look to the south, you see the round, white tip of Mt. Adams peering over those dusty brown hills, incongruous.

On that March day the chill air cracked and the sagebrush cast bright shadows on patches of snow as Don drove the Subaru down into the valley past big cattle ranches and their animals with thick winter coats, then smaller farms, past apple and pear orchards just starting to bud.

Our mother, Flo, rushed out to meet us as we pulled into the gravel driveway. She was dressed in her usual polyester pantsuit in bright colors. We hugged her thin frame in turn. Then, as she stood back to look at him, she brushed my brother's hair away from his face. "Don, I wish you would do something with your hair." (He had diplomatically removed the scarf and earrings.)

Don frowned. "Oh, Mom."

I thought Don's hair was beautiful—thick and dark and curly. I'd always wished I had inherited that head of hair from our mother. I might be wearing mine in the same long style. Instead, I wore my straight brown hair short, lately in the shag style Jane Fonda popularized in the movie Klute.

"Ok, you guys, come on in," she said, "I want you to see the new solar addition Tim put on the house."

Flo was never much of a housekeeper, but she was a genius at making this century-old farmhouse feel like home. We had bought the run-down three-acre place when I was nine, and remodeled it ourselves. Flo had filled it with antiques she'd collected from junk stores and the local dump. She always had to show us her new finds.

We visited for a while, then went out to say hello to our younger brothers Tim and Terry, whose four-wheel drive pickups were parked further up the driveway. The family home, which sat down in a hollow, had several outbuildings, all painted Swedish red with white trim like the house. The big old barn had been converted to a garage. Next to it was the chicken house surrounded by its chicken-wire pen. On the other side of the garage was the three-stall horse barn on which I'd painted a stylized picture of a horse years ago. Between them was what we called the doghouse, a rectangular structure that was once a shipping container. Someone had given it to my father years ago, and he set it on a slab and cut a door in it saying he'd have a place to go when he was in trouble with Flo. Over the years we'd fixed it up into a nice little apartment with electricity and running water and windows. All of us had used it at one time or another to get away from the house. I'd stayed there on summers home from college. For the past several years Tim and Diana had lived there together.

Tim answered the door, a tall, solid figure with a sparse beard and lanky brown hair. "Hey, how the fuck are you?" he said. We passed hugs around. "I've got some great pot this year. Smoke a joint?"

Don smiled. This was what he'd been waiting for. Yakima's hot dry summers are perfect for growing pot. Tim and Terry grew fine pot when it didn't get harvested prematurely in the middle of the night by one of their delinquent friends. One year they threw seeds around the farm indiscriminately and plants came up everywhere. One or two flourished in the middle of the gravel driveway.

We threw ourselves on the old foldout sofa. Terry passed out beers.

"So, what's the plan," I asked Diana. "What family events are we signed up for?"

"My girlfriends are giving me a shower tomorrow," she said.

"The wedding's on Saturday. It will be fun, you guys. We'll have dinner at the grange hall afterward, and Tim's friend Duane plays in a band. We can all dance. Tim's been taking dancing lessons." Diana was a dancer and a ballet teacher. I don't believe Tim had ever danced in his life or wanted to.

"What are you wearing," I asked.

Diana waltzed over to the closet and pulled out a plain white dress that was made interesting by the triangular pieces of green hanging like stalactites from the hem. It reminded me of a costume I'd seen in a performance of Peter Pan. "I made it myself," she beamed.

"It's beautiful," Don and I exclaimed in unison. We looked at Tim.

"Bought a suit," he shrugged.

"It's very handsome," said Diana, replacing the dress in the closet and pulling out a blue suit. "We had trouble getting it to fit in the shoulders. He's so wide."

Tim sucked at the joint and then smiled sheepishly.

"Now don't worry," Diana said, "you're going to look great."

"I have to go shopping," I said.

The next day my mother and I set out to find me a wedding outfit. Together we slogged through the department stores of my hometown, reliving painful memories of past shopping trips. I had never liked girls' clothes, and could only be induced to wear a style my mother called "tailored." Absolutely no frills or puckers. She'd understood. She'd never liked frilly clothes either. But she was five three and slender. I was five eight, and until my twenties, decidedly plump. More often than not, when I found the rare piece of clothing that suited me, it didn't come in my size. This had always mystified me. I knew there were plenty of other big-boned gals like me, but the people who designed clothes hadn't discovered us yet.

Sears was filled with nothing but polyester. Pants with elastic waistbands and no pockets. Over the years I'd developed a clothing checklist. I preferred natural fibers, and I wouldn't wear pants if they had no back pockets. "Don't be silly," my mother said.

I was indignant. "I intend to wear these pants more than one time," I reasoned. "Where will I put my wallet?"

At Montgomery Ward I insisted on starting in the men's department. I liked the color of a greenish suit on the display and convinced the clerk to let me try it on in the men's dressing room even though I knew what would happen. Those seventies-style men's pants were not made for my body. In the size that fit comfortably on my thighs, the waist was inches too big. These were not the kind of pants you could cinch up with a wide belt. They were the kind with the self-belt made of the fabric to fit a man's waist exactly. When I emerged from the dressing room my mother was not impressed. "Oh, Molly," was all she said. I knew she was right. I felt like a used car salesman.

We arrived at the Bon Marché irritated and frustrated. The Bon Marché was the Macy's of Yakima, Washington—clothes to aspire to. My attention span for shopping had always been short. And we had never shopped at the Bon when I was a kid. It was out of our price range.

I began to sift through racks of Misses slacks while Flo checked to see whether all the suits had skirts. Suddenly there it was. A rack of pants with back pockets. I was so happy it took me a minute to discover that the pockets were only half-pockets, not really big enough for a wallet. Why they do that I'll never understand. "Fuck, do they think putting regular-sized pockets in would cause us to grow penises?" I asked my mother.

"Why must you use that word," she scowled. "Try them on."

The pants did fit me better than the men's. I actually liked how they looked, even though I was still pissed about the pockets. "I hate giving money to a clothing industry that refuses to meet my needs," I said. But I was ready to compromise. I knew I'd never find anything better.

My mother returned with a navy polyester jacket, size 12. Women's jackets are always too tight in the shoulders or too loose around my waist, but this one wasn't bad. Before I could complain, she said, "I'll buy you the jacket."

Later she asked what shoes I'd be wearing. "Don't worry," I said, "I brought my Frye boots."

Flo insisted I come to the shower, even though the boys didn't have to. It was just as inane as I'd imagined. Diana was obliged to ooh and aah politely over every gift, no matter how useless. My mother had anticipated that I'd come to this heterosexual event empty-handed and resentful, so she'd bought a present from me. I was as surprised as Diana to discover I'd given her a set of wine glasses with their own rack. Flo never said a word about it.

The day of the wedding I was still searching for an appropriate shirt to wear with my new outfit. My father's closet had always served me well in the past. We're about the same size and he has short arms for a man. Whenever I'd visit, he'd send me away with several of his old shirts, which I'd wear with tails out over jeans until they began to fray right at the spots where my ample breasts, molded into a pointy-cupped bra, stuck out the farthest. I found a tasteful light blue number with a faint check. I was looking for a tie when Don breezed into the bedroom. He was wearing bright pink pants and a purple jacket, a pink polo shirt and platform shoes. He sashayed over to the dresser, pulled back his flowing hair and began putting dangly earrings in his pierced ears.

Flo was right on his heels, and she closed the door behind her. "Don," she wheedled, "I don't ask you for many things, but I'm asking you not to wear those earrings."

"Flo, stop making such a big deal out of it," he said in that artificially low voice he uses when he's annoyed. "I'm wearing the earrings."

My mother looked like she might cry. I wished I could make her feel better but I was sworn to defend my brother. "I don't understand why you must make things so hard for me," she said. She threw up her hands and walked out.

****

The wedding went off without a hitch. No one made rude comments about our gay apparel. Before the end of the evening when I had to admonish my drunken father to stop copping feels off the female guests, he had even said to me that he thought I looked "sharp" in his shirt and tie.

At the party when we were dancing, I felt the only wardrobe mistake I'd made was not to wear a bra. I hadn't thought pointy breasts would really go with my outfit (I had yet to discover the jockbra), so I wore an undershirt and let the breasts seek their natural level, about halfway to my waist. Jumping around with no support was painful but I didn't let that stop me.

Don and I were especially popular on the dance floor. I never lacked a partner; all the women loved me.

Women's Equality Day 1970

The feminist revolution in Yakima, Washington was not televised but I can testify that we were just as angry and militant as the sisters in New York who got all the press.

In the summer of 1970 I got a job as a reporter at the Yakima Herald-Republic, returning to my hometown to raise money to finance my senior year at college. I'd joined the feminist movement and I'd brought along my mom, Flo. She was already feminist material, a prolific writer of letters to the editor and an activist at heart. A look at my first pay check radicalized her further. She'd been making a third of my wage as the kind of secretary who actually runs the business while being paid as a typist.

At that time, newspaper reporter was a non-traditional job for women. It was ok for women to write for the women's section and the food section and to work as secretaries, but reporter was a man's job. The reporters at the YH-R had been organized into the Newspaper Guild and this was my first union job. I was elated, although I knew the Guild to be a weak union. I felt strongly that the secretaries and office workers ought to have a union too so I started talking up the idea of organizing. That got shut down fast! The office workers made it clear that they felt joining a union would be treasonous. They identified with the owners of the paper, at that time the descendants of its founding family. So, at the outset, this radical feminist succeeded in making enemies of the women workers. But they had been predisposed to dislike me from the beginning, especially one territorial secretary who saw me as a threat and whose put-downs had me hiding in the bathroom crying—the only time in my working career.

In the newsroom, the editor predictably assigned me to the women's page, where readers turned to discover which of Yakima's maidens were getting married that week. My job was to type up the wedding descriptions, which involved all of the fussy details like the cut of the bride's dress and color of the bridesmaids' frocks. In journalism school and as a student newspaper editor, I'd learned well the craft of editing. In my world, these unimportant details didn't belong in any story. My wedding paragraphs got shorter and shorter until—busted! Brides' mothers had begun calling my editor demanding to know why all the important details were missing. It turned out some people thought, and I venture to guess still think, that the color of the bride's mother's dress is big news. So my editor returned to writing up weddings and I went on to the news desk.

I did want to write about women, just not weddings. The features editor threw a few human-interest stories my way: a legally blind woman who'd become a pilot, a man who tatted, a dog that could ride on the back of a bike. I pitched a story to the news editor about where women in the Yakima Valley worked. Agriculture, mostly fruit orchards, was still the economic base of the region. My own grandmother had worked the line at a fruit processor and I'd picked apples in high school. I was truly interested in the demographics, but also wanted to investigate where we were *not* allowed to work. The editor thought it was a pretty good idea, but later reproached me, saying he had not known I was a feminist. How could I possibly write about this subject objectively, he wanted to know. Word sure got around fast.

When I pitched a story about the 50th anniversary of women's suffrage, they bit. Maybe I could find some real suffragists who'd been part of the struggle to win the vote! Washington women got the vote in 1910, the fifth state to give women the vote, ten years before the 19th amendment became law, so I figured there must have been a suffrage movement. My mother, who'd grown up in Yakima, wasn't born until 1913. She didn't know any suffragists, but I got a few leads and started searching nursing homes. I did find women to interview, but they had been mostly too busy raising kids and running farms to pay attention to politics, they said. This I dutifully reported in a feature article. If there had been militant suffragists in the early 1900s in Yakima, I failed to find them.

Yakima is a conservative place, infamous as the hometown of liberal Supreme Court Justice William O. Douglas. When FDR appointed Douglas to the Court, the Yakima paper disowned him as an outsider. Douglas had been born in Minnesota and raised in Yakima. Ironically, Douglas was nominated to the Court as a representative of the West, but he couldn't wait to get away from Yakima to seek his fortune. He wrote a book titled *Go East Young Man*.

Though I was undeniably a Yakima native, like Douglas I couldn't wait to get away from my hometown. But the prospect of living with my parents, working as a reporter and making trouble just for the summer seemed like fun. A small group of us formed Yakima's first National Organization for Women chapter, meeting at the home of a woman even older than my mom to document the inequality we experienced. We listed low pay, poor access to jobs and humiliating dress requirements, like having to wear hot pants to work as a waitress. There were restaurants and bars reserved for men only, and all those cultural expectations that we would serve our husbands, bear children and become homemakers. Also, everything we read placed the women's movement in New York City. We chafed at that version and wanted to show that sisterhood was powerful in little towns in the West too.

In the back seat of a VW bug on the way to the first meeting, the young woman sharing the seat with me whispered that her female lover had left her. Distraught, closeted, and with no community, she was looking for a friend to talk to. She saw in me something I had yet to see--I was a sister dyke. Later, I regretted that my own life experience was too sparse to understand or even to sympathize. I had yet to love and lose. I had yet to come out, even to myself.

While not well schooled in romance, by this time I was an experienced organizer, having planned and executed anti-war and women's liberation protests at college. I'd learned how to run a campaign and how to get media attention. I'd written and performed in guerrilla theater plays and given speeches, painted protest signs and silk-screened armbands. I'd participated in consciousness-raising and I was ready to act to change my world.

We aimed our first action at a restaurant where businessmen lunched that barred women. We had read about McSorley's bar in Manhattan, which had denied women entry for 116 years until it was forced to admit us that very summer. A journalist, Lucy Komisar, the first to test the judge's order, was doused in beer by jeering men. Our plan was to just walk in, sit down and demand service. We doubted beer dousing would follow, but who really knew what the reaction would be.

Resisting authority always made me nervous but also thrilled me. Just that spring we students had staged a giant strike and shut down Washington State University over racism. Flo had joined me at student demonstrations against the Vietnam War. My mother had saved me from threatened expulsion for moving off campus by making my case in a letter to the university president. Women's protests had led to the college aborting *in loco parentis* rules requiring us to wear dresses and to observe curfew. Old sexist ways were crumbling in our wake, making us feel the power of sister-hood. We were on a roll.

We had cased the restaurant and, as planned, six of us marched in and took a table right under the sign that read MEN ONLY. Flustered waiters ran to the manager for advice and we were asked to leave. Would they call the police to arrest us, we wondered. We weren't doing anything illegal, were we? We didn't leave but we did take up a table during the lunch hour while we were refused service. As it turned out, men didn't give up their privileges easily, but no dous-ing followed our restaurant protest and after some resistance we helped the restaurant to see the light. We won! I don't remember the names of the women, or how many visits it took, but I do remember the determination, the camaraderie and the elation we felt when the restaurant gave up its policy and served us all lunch.

That summer some of our other protests involved challenging dress codes by wearing pants to work (handy tip: start with cu-lottes) and pasting stickers that said "This Insults Women" on pub-lic signs and ads we deemed sexist (the ubiquity of these messages is hard for us to remember and for the young to imagine now.)

Our NOW group chose as its summer *coup de grâce* a rally to celebrate the 50th anniversary of women winning the right to vote on August 26, 1970. One day, at my desk at the newspaper, I got a call from the New York Times. They were doing a story about how feminist groups across the country were celebrating Wom-en's Equality Day. Elated, I eagerly catalogued our victories and detailed our plans for the rally.

In preparation for our celebration, the artist in our group made signs that we posted about town, others secured a sound system and a soapbox. We planned to rally in Franklin Park, near the city center. We arrived dressed in 1920s garb, imagining throngs of women all excited to speak out about their oppression publicly, but the hoped-for crowd didn't materialize as it had on the college campus. We gave a few short speeches, and then made the microphone available for other women to speak. Our rally ended when none stepped onto the soapbox. Among the lessons we learned: know your audience.

The next day I couldn't wait to see how my phone interview with the New York Times had come out. I rushed to the library to check out the paper and found the story—not in the women's section. Our rally may not have been televised, but our little group of Yakima activists made the Times!

Epilogue: We went on to change our world.

The Last Survivor

The posse didn't wait to start shooting as they drove their horses down into the wash where the Indians slept in their camp. The reward had been promised whether they were brought in dead or alive. It was easier to kill them all.

On a cold February day in the Nevada hinterlands, the battle raged for three hours, pitting 13 Indian men, women and children with few guns and little ammunition against 19 well-armed vigilantes. The Indians circled and danced a war dance. Then everyone fought. The women defended themselves and their children with spears and arrows. The little children threw rocks at the invaders.

One of the whites was killed as he rode forward with gun cocked when a girl stood, held up her skirts and flashed her genitals, smiling and moving forward in a weaving dance. As the attacker stared in astonishment, she dropped down and her brother shot him with the one bullet left in his gun.

The youngest baby was in a cradleboard on her mother's back when her 19-year-old mother, Wenegah, was shot and killed. Her head fell back into the snowy mud. The marauders heard her crying and retrieved her along with three other children who had run into the sagebrush.

That baby grew up to be Mary Jo Estep, the last surviving Indian of the last Indian massacre, in 1911. Of the four children who survived the massacre, the other three were sent to Indian schools and died the following year of tuberculosis. Mary Jo was taken in by a white family.

Mary Jo was about 18 months old when the posse ambushed the remnants of her tribe. Her grandfather, Shoshone Mike, had led the band across 300 miles of western desert in northern Nevada and California after refusing to go to a reservation.

Mary Jo knew little of this and did not remember it. When, in 1973, the Oregon writer Dayton O. Hyde wrote a book about her grandfather and the massacre, he speculated that the children might still be living. He learned of Mary Jo and then agonized about how to approach her and tell her the story of the massacre.

In 1911 Indians had no rights and were not considered to be human. White men could get away with killing Indians with impunity. It was easy to blame crimes on Indians, and that is what happened to Shoshone Mike. A cattle rustling gang whose leader was the son of a prominent judge blamed their crimes on Mike. A vigilante group formed with eyes on the reward money. Federal marshals also were after Mike and these posses began roaming the desert in northern Nevada looking for him.

Mike and his extended family evaded the posses for a year. But the winter of 1911 was the worst in a long time and, starving and tired, they were forced to camp in an unprotected spot where they were discovered.

Until Hyde wrote the book it was still said that Shoshone Mike had committed crimes and the killing of his family was justified. Mike's crime was that he wanted to live the nomadic life he had grown up with, camping every winter for 30 years on Rock Creek in southern Idaho and then moving to higher country for the summer season. The white man's fences, sheep and cattle, mining waste, and development made his family's lifestyle more and more difficult.

Hyde had been obsessed with the story of Shoshone Mike and his research included interviews with people who still remembered the massacre 60 years later. He traveled the route taken by

Mike and his family, even collecting remaining bones of the Indians and reburying them, since they had never been properly buried. Writing the book, he set the story straight. Mike and his family were innocent of the crimes whites accused them of. The murderers were never brought to justice; they were hailed as heroes by people in the surrounding towns. Hyde also uncovered evidence that Mike was Bannock, not Shoshone. His wife, Jennie, was Ute.

When she learned the story, Mary Jo's first reaction was to downplay it. "Most of my friends are non-Indians. I was raised in the white world," she said. Later she became a local celebrity of sorts in my hometown of Yakima, Washington, giving interviews and speaking to groups who wanted to hear her unique story.

Mary Jo Estep was raised by the family of the Fort Hall Indian reservation superintendent. She graduated from Central Washington College with a degree in music and spent 40 years teaching school before retiring in 1974. At the age of 82 in 1992, Mary Jo died in a nursing home because a nurse had given her the wrong medication and hospital staff determined that her non-resuscitate directive meant that they could not help her. The effects of the overdose could have been easily reversed. She took several hours to die and in that time her friends, who had come to pick her up for a party, surrounded and comforted her, but could not move the doctors to save her life.

"You look at what happened to her, and you could say that she died at the hands of the white man too," said Louis Jarnecke, one of her friends.

I still have the newspaper article telling of Mary Jo's death, and the book written about her grandfather, *The Last Free Man*. What they don't say is that Mary Jo Estep was a lesbian. She lived with her "long-time companion" Ruth Sweany for more than 50 years on Summitview Avenue in Yakima.

I met Mary Jo and Ruth through my mother who had organized a seniors' writing group in Yakima. My mom was interested in the history of our part of the world and she encouraged old people to tell and write their stories. She worked for the senior center there and for a time she produced a local TV program in which she interviewed old-timers and recorded their histories. The women told me they were part of a group called "Living Historians," and laughed saying, "At least we're still living!"

In 1980, my brother Don and his press, Hard Rain Printing Collective, printed a chapbook that includes the writing of all three: Mary Jo, Ruth, and my mother Florence Martin. Mary Jo's only piece in the chapbook chronicles an incident from her childhood of an old man who is lost and then found the next day by neighbors. Two of the published entries are by my mother. Ruth Sweany has four; three are poems, but the fourth is a prose piece that describes her life with Mary Jo, particularly when their friend Mabel comes to visit on Fridays. I think the friend must be Mabel George, another writer published in the chapbook.

A photo in the archive *Yakima Memory* from the Yakima Herald-Republic newspaper shows Mabel George (born January 8, 1899) at the piano, and another entry is titled Mabel George Children's Songs from 78 records, 1947. So Mabel was a musician and songwriter.

Ruth's story never mentions Mary Jo, but clearly the "we" in the piece refers to Ruth and Mary Jo as a couple. It's about the fun they have when their friend Mabel visits. They listen to music (a critique of modern loud disco music follows), they read poetry and plays to each other. They also write and produce plays, calling themselves "The Carload Players." Ruth writes that they even produced a couple of plays before an audience. This makes me wish their papers had been archived but I can find no evidence that they were saved.

These women rejoiced in each other's company. Ruth writes: "So our Fridays are always cheerful. Why not? We are doing things we enjoy, in a congenial group. After one of Mabel's visits the world stops going to the dogs and the sunshine comes out a little brighter."

Mary Jo died November 19, 1992. Ruth died November 28, nine days later. They were both buried in the Terrace Heights cemetery in Yakima. They chose identical gravestones.

Ruth and Mary Jo carved out their own woman-centered culture in the hostile environment of Eastern Washington before the advent of the modern women's movement and lesbian pride. Living lightly on the cultural landscape served them well.

Single Life

A	t 71, my father, Carroll, has been single for three years.
	"What's it like?" I ask. "Do you think it's different from single at 30, or 40?" I'm in a relationship at the moment, but considering the impermanence of modern lesbian relationships, this is information I intend to store for the future.

He looks at the sky and smoothes his gray mustache. "Probably not," he says.

We sit on the deck of his tiny trailer in a run-down resort in the California desert near the town of Needles. We are drinking vodka and grapefruit juice, perhaps a bit too fast. Vodka is his drink, not mine. He likes whiskey, he says, but his system just can't take it. Gin gives him an asthmatic reaction. But with vodka, he says, he's never had a hangover.

He has returned home from his travels to a stack of mail and he reads it as we talk, half-glasses perched on his nose. "This GD insurance company. I've been fighting with them for months. Who's this from? Oh, my friends the Carlsons. You remember Ben and Karen. They're coming to visit."

I move the stack of mail around and spot an envelope with recognizable handwriting. It is a card from my brother, Don, a notoriously poor correspondent.

"Dear Carroll," it says, "hope you are enjoying life in the desert. Everything is fine up here. I recently moved into a new apartment with a new roommate, a college student at the university. I'm working really hard on the Little Theater production of Cinderella, and work is going fine. Hope you had a good holiday."

"Have you talked to Don lately?" says Carroll.

"Not too long ago. He seems to be doing fine." I don't elaborate. Why should I explain, when Don does not, that he plays the part of the fairy godmother in Cinderella? I have met the new "roommate," a young man who clearly does not have his own bed.

Carroll leans back in the old metal deck chair and gives me a look, but asks no more questions. He has never wanted to know the details of my brother's private life, nor mine, and we have never told him in so many words.

"That was something, Liberace dying," he says.

"Yes, it was sad." What I think is Don hasn't had the test. I'm terrified that he is positive. For a moment I wish I could talk to Carroll about it.

"I don't think it's right that people should be able to hide the cause of death like he did," he says.

"I think it was a terrible thing they did to him," I say. "He should have been allowed to die in peace." Carroll makes some more protests, but he's not much of a fighter and I don't feel very argumentative at the moment.

I go back to riffling through his mail. "What's this?" I say, turning over an envelope with flowery handwriting.

He has saved the good stuff for last. "From Irma," he says, opening the envelope and scanning the card quickly. He passes it to me.

A teddy bear in a lacy bed looks forlornly out from the card. "I think of you daily and miss you enormously," it says.

Somehow I have the feeling this thinking and missing is not reciprocal. "How sweet." I take a swig.

I suspect Carroll had been seeing Irma before my mother died, but I try not to hold that against her. Carroll was a little too pushy about it was all, wanting everything to be okay. He insisted I meet her, and the one time I did, she seemed perfectly nice. She told me Carroll was the first man who'd appealed to her in fifteen years.

"You're obviously putting some distance between you and Irma," I say, pulling myself out of the chair.

"She drinks too much for me," he says. "I tell her I think she's an alcoholic and she doesn't like that."

"I was just getting up to freshen our drinks," I say, thinking Irma's habit must be serious. For as long as I can remember, Carroll has had a drinking problem. Cracked up two company cars. Always had a pint under the front seat. During my childhood many a dinner was eaten in the tension of his absence.

I duck into the trailer's kitchen. "Are you trying to cut down?" I ask through the screen door as I assemble juice, vodka and ice.

"The doctor bugs me about it. I try to watch myself," he says, "but when I'm with Irma I drink more. It's harder to control. I don't want to get mixed up with an alcoholic."

"I think that's smart," I say, resisting the burden of my mother's anguish.

The trailer is spare as a monk's quarters. Only one picture— of my brother Terry's children—is displayed on the kitchen table. There are no pictures of my mother or the four of us kids, and none of her things are here. She collected old things, I believe because she wanted a link with history. When she died, Carroll ignored our objections and sold the farm and the contents of our childhood home. "What do I want with things?" he'd said. "I'll die soon anyhow." Then he bought a pickup and went on the road. Later, he tried to make it up to me. "Take it," he would say about objects I expressed interest in, but there was nothing I really wanted then.

I walk back out, hand him a drink, sit across from him and pick out another large envelope. "Who's this from?"

He smiles, devilishly I think. "That's Eleanor, my South Dakota girlfriend."

This one has a serious message lettered on the front.

"I hope only that you can love me just the way I am," it says. Inside a handwritten message adds, "I do hope someday this can be so."

"What does this mean?" I ask.

He ponders the card. "Can't figure it. She's a pretty hippy gal. Maybe she thinks I want her to lose weight."

"Why would she think that?"

"Oh, I've commented on it," he says. A "big boned" survivor of years of badgering from thin parents, I decide I'd rather not get into this.

"Who's your girlfriend here, the one your neighbors were razzing you about?" I ask.

"Blanche? She's a class above the rest in this place. Likes to have a good time. Likes to dance."

I have never thought of Carroll as particularly handsome. But in his set he is the belle of the ball. Last night at the local resort dance he never lacked a partner. Women approached me and asked, "Is that your father? He sure is cute." I haven't seen such flirting since my generation of lesbians all discovered each other.

We look out on the slough, where fishers glide by in rowboats toward the Colorado River. Fish aren't biting tonight. The local colony of ducks flap wings and chase each other in a frenzy of mating. I wonder why my father and I so often seem to find ourselves in the company of mating animals. I hope he senses my discomfort and doesn't call attention to this ritual.

"The ducks are sure sexy tonight," he says. "'Let's chase each other 'round the room tonight.' Ever heard that song? They played it at my sister Jesse's fiftieth wedding anniversary."

"It doesn't look like much fun to me," I say, watching a drake hold a hen under the water.

"Probably is for him," he says.

"So what about sex?" I plunge in. "Do these women you're dating like sex?"

He's pleased I asked this question, pleased to have a chance to talk about it, I think. "Hell, yes, sure they do. Irma can take it or leave it though. She can be cold but I don't care about that. I was never one to demand sex. I never in my life said 'I'm not getting any here, so I'm going somewhere else.'"

I've finished my drink and want another, but am afraid to break this train of thought. "What about Eleanor?" I ask.

"Now Eleanor is a different story. She's quite a bit younger than me—fifties I guess. you know those middle-aged women, they're sexy."

"Yes I do," I say, feeling middle-aged. "So you just returned from a tryst."

"Well, you know my cousin Buford died. I had to go up to Sturgis. But the funny thing about Eleanor, she doesn't want anyone to know. She's real involved in the church, and she's afraid someone will find out about us. I kind of get a kick out of it. She kicks me out by five o'clock so they won't see me there in the morning. But she is something in bed. I tell her 'If your church friends only knew what goes on in this house…'"

I have developed a sudden interest in a broken thumbnail and am picking at it intently.

"Eleanor thinks I'm really sexy," Carroll says. "But I'm really not. You know, she expects too much of me. They all think I'm sexy. I can't figure out why." I rip the thumbnail off and my thumb begins to bleed.

"So what about Eleanor? Are you getting serious?" I ask, sticking the thumb in my mouth to stop the bleeding.

"Naw. I know she'd like to get married, but I'm not gonna do it. Don't you worry. I don't intend to get married again."

"What makes you think I'd worry? You're an independent person. You can make your own decisions."

I hug myself. The sun has gone down and the evening is suddenly cool.

"Well, what do you say we get cookin'?" Carroll raises his furry black eyebrows at me, gets up and moves into the trailer.

The prospect does not excite me. His bachelor diet of sausage, Spam and fried potatoes gives me heartburn. "Let's try something different tonight," I say, opening the refrigerator, which contains little more than ingredients for various alcoholic concoctions. I pull out the biggest thing in there, a heavy rectangular package. "What's this?"

"Government cheese," he says. "They give it away to senior citizens every two weeks at the surplus store. I want you to take that with you when you go."

"No thanks. I could never eat all this. I live alone, remember?"

"No, I want you to take that." He is using his sergeant voice. "I can get plenty more where that came from."

"No, really, I don't like processed cheese. I would never eat it."

"You take that," he insists. "Give it to your friends."

"Look, I appreciate the offer," I say. "Maybe we can cook something with it tonight. Does your oven work?"

He finds some matches and kneels down in front of the little propane stove while I start turning knobs on and off looking for the one that controls the oven. "I never did figure out how to use this thing," he says.

I am watching as he works at lighting it when the air around his head explodes with a whoosh. He is knocked backwards and ends up sitting on the floor against a counter.

"Dad, Dad," I yell. "Are you okay?" I get down in front of him and his eyes finally focus on me. I can see his thick eyebrows and lashes have been singed. He rubs the melted nubs of hair on his arm. I discover I am crying.

"Knocked the piss out of me, but I'm okay." He looks puzzled.

"I'm kind of upset," I blurt out. "I'm afraid Don might have AIDS. I can't stand to lose him, too."

Carroll's face betrays no anger, only resignation. "He's always gone for men, hasn't he?"

"Yes," I say, and more to atone for indiscretion than anything else, I add, "and I love women."

"I don't understand it," he says, "but I'm glad you've been quiet about it."

I give him a hand up, then wipe my eyes quickly on my shirt sleeve. He smooths the ruff of gray hair around his bald head and tucks in his shirt. I decide to cook something on top of the stove.

"Hey, I want you to see something," he says. "Look at my gold nugget." He pulls what looks like a huge nugget from his pocket. It is attached to a gold chain.

I'm immediately skeptical. One of his favorite pastimes is making up stories about found objects or people he sees in passing, or family history. Years pass and fiction melds with truth. "Where did you get this?" I laugh.

"Well, now, some people might think this is strange," he says, eyeing me as he places it in my hand. "You know your mother had a lot of dental work done over the years and she had all her teeth pulled the week before she died. This is made from her gold teeth. I want you to take it."

How the Lesbians Invaded Bernal Heights

We had been powerless tenants, evicted with no recourse, and then we became agents of displacement. There was no in between.

My collective household of four lesbians had found a place on Castro Street, one of those original Victorians with high ceilings and elaborate wood trim, an abandoned coal fireplace and a parlor whose big sliding doors opened to double the size of the room. It was rumored that the apartment had come up for rent because the previous tenants had been busted for selling weed and were all in jail. We embellished the story to claim that the famous Brownie Mary had lived there. She may not have lived there, but she had certainly been there in spirit. Mary dispensed her marijuana brownies in the neighborhood when pot was still very much illegal. It was the seventies; the Castro was becoming a gay men's mecca. During our time there a housepainter engaged to paint our building turned tricks in the building's storage room. He painted that building for months.

We fondly remember political gabfests at shared dinners, Seders in which we sang all the way through, inventive costumes at Halloween parties (in the year of Anita Bryant I came as a lesbian recruiter.) For a time our costume *du jour* at home was simply a vest, a way to show off a billowing bush and legs as thickly furred as animal pelts (we were hairy and proud!). We danced and sang along to Stevie Wonder and Lavender Jane Loves Women. There was much laughing and also much crying. Passionate love affairs abounded. Creating a new culture calls for invention. We experimented with nonmonogamy and polyamory. We felt we were on the cutting edge of a cultural transformation.

When the gay male couple from LA bought the three-unit building in 1978, they immediately evicted us. We had no recourse; rent control was still a few years off. We found a smaller apartment on 29th Street just off Mission in the neighborhood we now call La Lengua at the foot of Bernal Heights. Our landlords were butchers, brothers who ran a shop on Mission Street right next to Cole Hardware. Weirdly, the buildings on 29th Street and Mission Street were connected. Our apartment above the butchers' always smelled like dead meat, like something had died in the walls.

(That building was damaged by the 2016 fire that laid waste to Cole Hardware, the Playa Azul restaurant and the handsome turreted Greystone Hotel, which had anchored the corner of 29th and Mission since 1897 and was home to the 3300 Club, the poets' bar.)

We liked the location—right behind the Safeway parking lot and across the street from the Tiffany gas station. Pauline's Pizza was just across Mission and Mexican restaurants like Mi Casa and El Zocalo proliferated. I quaffed beer at El Rio, a mixed gay bar. I bought my work clothes at Lightstone's, the shop owned by Paula Lichtenstein. The post office was right next-door. The building's ground floor held a printer's shop (it's now a pot club) and the second floor was just a big meeting room that was rented by Union Women's Alliance to Gain Equality (Union WAGE) which allowed other organizations like Tradeswomen, Gays for Nicaragua, Lesbians Against Police Violence and the Briggs Initiative opposition to meet there.

My collective of four politically active dykes—me, two Ruths and a Pam—was happy. We cooked and ate together and invited interesting people to share dinner. Jews and militant atheists ruled. I learned about Jewish culture. The Christmas tree was relegated to a bedroom. It was bliss, except that with visiting lovers and pets (one a gigantic great Dane) and parents and friends the place was just too small. Finally we decided that we either had to pool our money and buy a bigger place or split up the collective.

We were earnest idealists; we were gay activists; we had just lived through the horrors of the Moscone Milk murders and Jonestown, the I Hotel eviction and the election of Reagan. We were committed to live ethically and, even in the midst of what felt like political chaos, we fervently believed we could change the world, ending US imperialism, racism, police violence, and discrimination against women and gays. We were part of a collective movement that emphasized cooperation and consensus decision-making, a radical departure from capitalist organization that resulted only in winners and losers.

We tried to visualize a new living situation, listing our requirements for the ideal house. Ruth had to have a garden. I desperately needed a garage to store my electrical contracting tools and supplies. We had to be close to public transportation. We didn't want a fixer upper; no one had time for that and I was the only tradeswoman. We were committed to collective living and we also fantasized about eventually dispensing with private property. What if we could donate the place to a land trust so that our dream of a lesbian nation could live on into future generations?

We negotiated a contract. What would happen if one of us died or ended up in jail or for some reason couldn't make her payment? How would we sell and buy shares in the building? What if we needed to make repairs or improvements? We listed all contingencies. We were good at processing—we were lesbians!

We imagined a larger single-family house, one with four real bedrooms, but then when we found the three-unit place on the south side of Bernal Hill our imaginations blossomed. We would no longer have to share one bathroom and one kitchen, but we could still cook and eat together whenever we wanted. Instead of negotiating for time to call each of our telephone trees on our shared phone, each would have her own phone.

The listing price was $135,000, an incomprehensible amount. A hundred thousand then felt like a billion now—you couldn't get your head around it. Still, we dug deep and came up with the down payment, only because Pam was able to borrow money from her family. Then we wrote up a new contract to repay Pam by the month. We got pretty good at writing contracts.

As soon as we took possession in 1980, our place in the property hierarchy changed. We became agents of displacement. All three of the units were occupied. Each of us had to evict tenants before we could move in and none of us could afford to pay both rent and mortgage for long. Oh the contradictions! I talked with the couple in "my" unit, offering to help them find a new place. Our exchanges were friendly and civil, and they soon found new housing. But Ruth couldn't even get the tenant in "her" unit to open his door, though she could hear him spewing expletives from the other side. She resorted to lawyers and eviction notices.

We weren't the first lesbians to move to Bernal Heights. Political activist Pat Norman and her large family lived up the block. A lesbian couple had settled just around the corner. But there were four of us, and with friends and lovers coming and going we were hard to ignore. People in the neighborhood noticed. Homophobia took the form of nasty notes left on car windshields and DYKES graffiti on the building. Two neighbors who grew up on the block, guys about my age, made it clear they understood what we represented—a lesbian invasion. Years later, when our relationship had grown friendlier, one of them confided, "We were watching you."

As much as we wanted to live collectively, the house on Richland restricted collectivity. Having separate apartments led to fewer shared meals and less knowledge of each other's daily lives. I retreated into the dreaded merged lesbian couple relationship. After a few years the original members began to sell their shares and move out while others bought in. At the cusp of the 80s our world changed. That frantic hopeful creative collective time was ending.

But we are still here. Since the birth of our dyke-owned dream, we have aided the lesbian colonizing of San Francisco and particularly Bernal Heights. With each refinancing (too numerous to count) and buyout, our property underwrote the purchase of new female-owned houses. When we started, four single women buying property together was rare and suspect by financiers (women had only just been able to get credit in our own names.) Tenants-in-common was not a typical way to hold property. Since then it's been adopted by the real estate industry as a way to make buying of increasingly expensive property possible for groups of unrelated individuals.

We were agents of change, the leading edge of a new wave of homeowners in the Mission and Bernal Heights. But change is not new to our neighborhood. As one of the authors of a pictorial history of Bernal Heights, I researched its historic demographics. Indigenous Ohlones had lived in a thriving settlement at the mouth of nearby Islay Creek. Irish squatters displaced the Mexican land grant Californios. European immigrants made homeless by the 1906 earthquake and fire moved earthquake shacks here and built new homes. Southern Italians colonized the north side of the hill. Germans, Swedes and Italians built churches here for ethnic congregations. Mexicans and Blacks found a neighborhood free of racist covenants and restrictions, although Bernal was not outside redlining boundaries. During the economic downturn starting in 2008, big banks (locally based Wells Fargo gained our enduring hatred) evicted scores of homeowners, most of them people of color. Now houses on this block are selling for millions and the techies are moving in.

The life we built is changing. Pat Norman retired, sold her house and moved to Hawaii. My long-time friend around the corner, the first lesbian I met in the neighborhood, sold her house and moved to Oakland. And now, in 2018, I've sold the apartment where I've lived for 37 years in order to colonize a neighborhood in Santa Rosa.

Our particular experiment may be ending, but the neighborhood is still full of dykes. In Bernal Heights, lesbians found an affordable generally accepting environment. At one time I heard that the neighborhood was home to more woman-owned property than any neighborhood in the country or in the world. Who knows; that may still be true.

Still Standing

Ruth S was the first to live in the top-floor apartment after our collective household of four lesbians bought the three-unit building on Richland Avenue in San Francisco's Bernal Heights neighborhood. She confided that in big storms it felt like a boat on the sea. You could get seasick with the rocking.

I've now lived in all the flats—A, B and C—and I can testify that Ruth was not exaggerating. One afternoon, lying on my bed in the far southern reaches in the lowest unit of the four-story building, I could feel a gentle rocking. It might have rocked me to sleep had I not been worrying about its source. There was no wind. I could see the blue sky from my window. Later I asked my partner Donna, whose bedroom was on the top floor in the far northern corner, what she thought might have caused it.

"Sex," she answered rather sheepishly. "We were having sex."

As amusing as this was, to have knowledge of my house partners' sexual habits by just lying on my bed in a distant part of the building, it concerned me greatly about the constitution of our home. Was it going to fall down? And if so, when?

With this question in mind, I invited one of my building inspection coworkers to come by and have a look (I didn't tell him about the sex.) I just felt there was something terribly wrong with the way this building had been constructed. What could the problem be and how might we fix it? Of course, he had no idea. The walls had long been closed and I didn't at that time have the energy for a big project that included opening walls and inspecting structural members. But I had at various times opened pieces of walls to pull in low voltage wiring or to try to parse out what the builders might have had in mind.

I first moved into the lowest unit, Apartment A, in 1980 with my lover Nancy. We noticed immediately that the kitchen floor's angle was far steeper than, say, the angle of repose for raw eggs. Whenever we dropped anything liquid it would run so quickly from one side to the other that the cook would have to dive to the floor in order to catch it before it disappeared into the framing.

The interior had been finished, but badly. We could see that the previous owner had covered the kitchen with quarter-inch sheet-rock, painting it all a bright yellow so that no one would notice. The sheetrock even covered the wooden window trim, making you wonder what he had been trying to hide. Nancy was a carpenter and I an electrician. We couldn't stand not knowing what was behind the quarter-inch. And we wanted to even out the kitchen ceiling, which had a mysterious soffit hanging over the entrance door. One Saturday while I was away at a tradeswomen meeting Nancy demo'd the soffit (it had seemed like a simple quick job) and I returned to a kitchen full of rats' nest material and rat poison boxes from the 1920s. After that we did not open walls with such abandon.

But later I did have to open the kitchen wall. Investigating a short, I opened electrical boxes trying to figure out where the kitchen outlet was fed from, with no success. I finally pulled off a piece of the quarter-inch sheetrock thinking I'd find a pipe or a piece of electrical cable leading to another outlet. Instead I found that someone (clearly not an electrician) had run not cable but two wires stapled directly to the wooden original kitchen wall and then covered the whole mess with the quarter-inch sheetrock. The wires disappeared under the sheetrock. Where did they go? There was no telling. This discovery horrified me. No electrician or anyone concerned with fire hazard would ever have done such a thing. It meant that we could hang a picture on the wall and short out a circuit or start a fire. But there was nothing to be done then. I patched the sheetrock and made a mental note to never hang a picture on that wall. It wouldn't be till 20 years later that I would have the money and gumption to open the walls to see what was really inside.

After closing up the kitchen wall and vowing not to think about the wiring, Nancy and I lived together in Apartment A for a couple of years before experiencing a devastating breakup involving our mutual best friend who lived across the street. Nancy was the first of our original collective of four to be bought out. I vowed never to buy property with a lover again and I stuck with my vow for many years.

Our collective had thought long and hard about all the possibilities of home ownership, drawing up a contract that spelled out how collective members would be bought out and how new owners would be chosen, how much monthly "rent" would cost and the amount of homeowners' dues. What we failed to understand was the concept of equity as it relates to real estate. Our idea was that each member's equity was equal to all the money she had put into the pot, including monthly mortgage payments. None of us had owned real estate. We didn't understand that most of the payment went toward interest on the loan. So we ended up buying Nancy out for more than her actual equity. But it was a good lesson. We became real estate mavens.

Then I moved into Apartment B. At the culmination of a lovely housewarming dinner, I turned on the coffee maker and all the lights went out. The electrician's house, my friends laughed, like the unshod cobbler's kids. That was the start of a long journey of discovery that would shock my electrical sensibilities and make me wonder why the building had not burned down in an electrical fire long before my time here.

Wires live inside walls and ceilings and so without opening up walls it would be very difficult to understand what was going on, but I could surmise that the apartment was served by only a single circuit. That in itself was troubling and there was no way of knowing the quality of the work or the condition of the wiring. In the 1990s, my job as an electrical inspector required me to explain to other homeowners and business owners that their faulty electrical wiring could cause a fire. Every time I said, "If you don't fix this problem, a fire could result," I would think to myself, "My own home could burn down!" I didn't know the half of it.

Over the years collective members sold their shares, others bought in and sold out until I was the only one left. It wasn't until the year 2000 that I had the time and inclination, and also a partner who wanted to get her hands dirty, to begin to open walls and really see the structure. What we found was worse than anything I'd imagined: no studs in half of the third-story apartment, bearing walls cut off at the garage level causing the building to sag in the middle (the answer to the raw egg question), a monstrous electrical fire hazard.

As we deconstructed the building, we kept wondering why it was so oddly shaped, why construction methods differed from floor to floor and room to room, why floors were different heights in adjacent rooms, why floor and ceiling joists sometimes went north and south, sometimes east and west, why when wall coverings were removed we could see sky through cracks in the exterior walls.

Then one day when I was standing across the street looking at the building I had an epiphany. Our home was never a plan in some architect's mind. It was a collection of buildings set on top of one another, cut off, pushed together, raised up, and without benefit of removal of siding, spiked together with a few big nails. Suddenly all the mysteries we'd catalogued made sense. Our four-story three-unit building had probably begun life as a homesteader's shack in 1893, the year of the newspapers that had been pasted on interior redwood plank walls as insulation. As we uncovered the walls, we read stories in the *San Francisco Call*. 1893 was a very interesting year.

Remodeling the building with the help of our tradeswomen sisters took us nearly a decade. I had always wanted to build a house and that dream was realized by *rebuilding*—a far more challenging project.

Gay Man Stabbed in Heart Survives

"Gay Man Stabbed in Heart Survives," read the front-page headline in the BAR, a gay newspaper I picked up while strolling on Castro Street.

Then I looked at the picture. It was my old college roommate Larry Johl. I recognized him immediately from his long very blond hair. As students at Washington State University we had lived together in the Rosa Luxemburg Collective in Pullman, Washington, a little town near the Idaho border. (Rosa Luxemburg, whose giant portrait we painted on our dining room wall, was a Polish revolutionary socialist theoretician who was assassinated in 1919—our hero.)

That was in 1973-74 before we had each decamped to the gay mecca of San Francisco. We had been in touch, and I had once been to Larry's apartment on Broderick Street, furnished tastefully in deco style with castoff furniture and cheap (but not cheap-looking) window treatments.

Our get-together in San Francisco in the late 70s had revealed that Larry worked at a boring, low-paid office job in some bureaucracy. He described himself as a snow queen, meaning that he preferred to date Black men. He had a cute, angelic-looking boyfriend whose picture graced his bedroom chest of drawers.

When I thought back to our collective living arrangement at Rosa's, in a huge house with 11 others, I remembered Larry had a thing for Black men even then. It was Larry who introduced us to the music of the gay icon Sylvester. How did Larry discover him? How did Larry discover gay culture? It seemed like he had emerged a full-blown raging queen from his tiny desolate hometown of Soap Lake, in the eastern Washington desert, the middle of nowhere. He told me that as a kid he'd been a big fan of Elizabeth Taylor and had filled secret scrapbooks with her pictures cut from magazines. Perhaps he'd been a queen from birth, living testimony for the argument for nature over nurture.

Larry didn't come out to us at Rosa's but we knew. He personified all the stereotypes—limp wrists, lilting voice, scathing wit and the neatest room in the house. In the collective, Larry was the roommate most concerned with beauty and fashion.

Our Welsh roommate Keith couldn't believe Larry's wealth of information about popular culture. "He never reads. How can he know so much?" True, we seldom saw Larry studying. How did he pass his exams?

For that matter, none of us was very focused on school. We spent most of our time trying to upend the status quo. We were desperate to change the direction of national politics, refusing to pay the federal phone tax that funded war and staging die-ins at ROTC functions. The FBI came knocking at the door after Larry sent a threatening letter to President Nixon. I don't believe he was arrested. He had only put in writing what we were all thinking.

Larry was central to our countercultural and political activities, excelling in tasks organizational. His specialty was the media blitz. With our dissident friends, we had formed the League for the Promotion of Militant Atheism (the LPMA) in response to a student Christian crusade. The Jesus freaks' slogan was "One Way," and they'd proselytize holding up an index finger. It was annoying as hell. Our slogan became "No Way," our sign a zero made with index finger and thumb. During registration week when students poured into the student union and all the organizations set up their wares at the entrance, Larry sat at our table and showed slides of all the churches in town, a tape of Elton John's *Burn Down the Mission* playing continually in the background. Then, when we staged a debate about the existence of god, Larry took on media/outreach and managed to fill the auditorium to capacity.

I think my brother Don would say Larry brought him out of the closet. Don didn't live with us at Rosa's but he visited frequently. In those days our sexual identities weren't so clearly defined. We all experimented with gay as well as straight sex, although in retrospect the women seemed much freer than the men. The women swung like kids on a new play set, while the men tended to gravitate to one corner or the other of the sandbox. Neither Larry nor my brother Don was ever interested in women at the orgies we sponsored. They would carry on afterwards dishing male anatomical details, which I invariably missed.

After I saw his picture on the front page of the BAR, I called Larry. He was out of the hospital. He told me he had been cruising Buena Vista Park at 2 a.m. when he was attacked and stabbed. His attackers then tried to pull off his leather clothes. He was saved by a punk couple who got him to the hospital just in time. He had lost almost all the blood in his body. The gay bashers were never caught.

I asked Larry what he intended to do next. He said he was just going to live life as he had, maybe with more passion and vigor. "I could get hit by a bus tomorrow," he told me cheerfully. He figured all the time in the future was free. He had been spared death, for the time being.

By that time in the early 80s we knew about AIDS but there was no test available yet and of course there was no treatment. Gay men were just dying. You would see your friend, a young man you sang with or worked out with, looking healthy and vibrant. Then he would get a diagnosis and within weeks he would be dead.

When I asked my brother Don to tell me his memories of Larry, he remembered that they had seen each other in the late 80s. By that time Larry must have known he was HIV positive. He told Don that when he died he wished to be cremated and he wanted someone to fling his ashes from a window of the 24 Divisadero, the bus that took him from his neighborhood in the Western Addition to the gay bars in the Castro. He said he wanted all the queens to prance behind the bus and stomp him into the pavement with their platform shoes.

I never saw Larry again, and when I tried to call, his number had been disconnected. I couldn't find mention of him anywhere, though I was pretty sure he had died of AIDS. The BAR had been printing obits for gay men since 1972, but it never published his. Did he, like many gay men, go back home to die? That was hard for me to imagine. Did he die alone or did he have a network of friends to care for him? Was he one of the ones who perished within weeks? Don and I felt negligent, that we had not come to his aid when he was dying. I sure hope someone did.

Eventually I found a notice of his death in the Ephrata, Washington paper, a slightly larger small town near Soap Lake. He had died in 1990. He was 39. But there were no details and so I just had to imagine his last years and days. Also in the Ephrata obits I found a Carl A. Johl, born 1914, who died in 2009 at the age of 94. I guess Carl was Larry's father.

When some of the Rosa Luxemburg Collective roommates reunited again after 35 years, I had to come out to them as a lesbian. Then it fell to me to explain Larry's fate to this assemblage of straight folks. I fear I failed.

Lesbians and gay men lived in different but overlapping cultures, which we were continually inventing back in the 1970s and

80s. As a close student of lesbian feminist culture, I had no trouble discoursing on its development. But I was instantly aware that I didn't really know the culture Larry lived in. How to explain his cruising escapades and his obvious sluttiness? The story seemed to suggest that he was responsible for his own demise, at least as I imagined my straight comrades might see it. We were a progressive bunch who believed in free love and revolution, rejecting nuclear war as well as the nuclear family. Still, I sensed disapproval in their shocked emailed responses.

Or was it something like envy? Larry had found himself in San Francisco and he was finally free to live an openly gay life. I think he was happy. Perhaps he and I were two collective members who succeeded in transcending the conventional lifestyle that we countercultural dissidents had all worked so hard to reject.

****

The 24 Divisadero is a crosstown bus route that goes from the rich white neighborhood of Pacific Heights clear down to the poor Black neighborhood of Bayview-Hunters Point. It was the bus that for decades carried me from my neighborhood in Bernal Heights to the Castro to gay bookstores, bars, demonstrations, and film festivals at the Castro Theater. My wife and I would often stop for a beer at Harvey's on the corner of 18th and Castro just to cruise the street crowd through its big windows.

The scene is still vibrant and colorful, but there are times when walking in the Castro I sense the ghosts of the young men who died of AIDS. Then I'm overwhelmed with grief, so very aware of all that we have lost. I share this grief with an entire generation of people who lived through the AIDS years. Our community was stabbed in the heart, but we have survived.

Nuns Take the Castro

When sing-along movies became a big thing in the early 2000s they would sell out little-used movie houses. People dressed in theme costumes waited in long lines with their kids to get in at venues all over the country. In San Francisco the place to sing along with musicals was and still is the Castro Theater, the 1920s-era movie theater in the heart of the gay district. What could be better than flaunting your clever musical movie costume on Castro Street?

It helped if you knew all the words to all the songs. My girlfriend Barb, a survivor of Catholic schools whose first love had always been nuns, knew all the words to all the songs in "The Sound of Music", and when it came to the Castro she insisted we go as nuns. I was game but, having grown up Protestant, clueless.

My only experience with nun habits prior to our adventure had been the Sisters of Perpetual Indulgence. The Sisters, a group of flamboyant gay men, formed in the 1970s partly as an antidote to the anti-gay misogynistic backward teachings of the Catholic Church. They dress in outrageous nun costumes and have worked hard to make the AIDS crisis visible when it was ignored by the powers that be. I love the Sisters, still a presence in San Francisco and especially the Castro. It was at a Sisters event in the early 80s called Holy Daze (including a mix of religious cults) where I learned about the plagues of Egypt and how to counteract the curses by declaring *feh!* and flipping wine at one another until you are covered with wine. Our plagues were things like union busting and Reaganomics. On the stage was set a long table with 12 "apostles" including The Cosmic Lady who we would see walking in the

Mission handing out flyers with a picture of the Milky Way and an arrow with the slogan: "You Are Here."

Barb took charge of the costumes, which she announced would reflect the Catholic order of her hometown in southern Indiana, the nuns who were her teachers in Catholic schools. Her own aunt had taken the veil and so Barb knew exactly what the wimples, scapulars and associated habit parts looked like. No Sisters of Perpetual Indulgence influence here with elaborate headpieces and drag queen makeup. We would look like the real thing, authentic representatives of the Order of St. Benedict from the convent on the hill in Ferdinand, Indiana.

I was dispatched to second-hand stores in the Mission to pick up long-sleeved black dresses to serve as tunics. That was the easy part. On a stormy Saturday we assembled material to create the wimples, veils and coifs. Barb, a crafty gal who was always good at making things, dove into the project with great zeal. Perhaps she was finally realizing a long-held dream: some part of her had always wanted to be a nun, or at least to be seduced by one. My own part in this play was becoming clearer.

We worked all day on the project and when it was finished we were delighted with the results. Modeling the habit put me in touch with its medieval origins. The wimple covered my ears and blocked my hearing, cloistering me from the world.

On the day of the sing-along we got dressed early so we could show our friend Pat (also an ex-Catholic) our new personas. The final touch—black leather combat boots, just visible below the long tunics. In the spirit of both the Sisters of Perpetual Indulgence and the Sisters of St. Benedict we chose our names as brides of Christ. I was Sister Mary Mollybolt (in reference to my tradeswoman background) and Barb was Sister Barbwire. As it turned out, we should have reversed our names, as I was to be the bad nun and she the good. An important part of my costume was the wooden ruler I carried, slapping it on my palm menacingly. Barb couldn't stop laughing; she was so delighted to finally be a nun.

Pat took our picture before we tripped over to the Castro. We made a great team, and I wondered if nuns teamed up in pairs the way cops do to interrogate or dispense punishment. I was getting into my role as the bad nun.

The Castro District is a place where adults can show up in just about any costume and not cause so much as a second look. Even on days when nothing special is happening, the Castro can seem like Halloween. We felt right at home strolling the street as nuns, along with others dressed as characters in the "Sound of Music"— the children dressed in curtains, even a mountain range.

We had arrived with plenty of time to eat dinner and so dropped into a local eatery. The other patrons seemed shocked by our presence. We thought it was obvious that we were fake nuns. After all, the combat boots were visible elements. And this *was* the Castro. But our nun costumes sent some of the Catholics at this place back to their trauma-filled childhoods. They were really disturbed by my ruler. As we stood waiting for a table, people began approaching us and telling us stories of their encounters with the nuns and the Catholic Church. One woman recalled being hit with such a ruler as a kid. A man told of his abusive Catholic education in Germany. We became a means for these people to talk about the trauma they'd suffered at the hands of the Catholic Church. They had to tell us their stories. They couldn't stop. I was fascinated.

The scandal of priests' child abuse in the Catholic Church had been ongoing and the Boston Globe would break the big story about child sexual abuse in the Boston archdiocese shortly after our foray into the Castro as nuns. But we got a sense of the underlying culture that night. Nuns are a powerful representation of the Catholic Church and the abuse it dealt to its parishioners.

****

The sing-along was all that we'd imagined. We got to belt out *How Do You Solve a Problem Like Maria?* and all the other songs. We didn't enter the costume contest. Compared to all the other imaginative costumes, the abundant nuns were rather boring. The mountain range consisting of nine mountains won first prize. We had great fun, but the most memorable part of my night as a nun was our inadvertent unleashing of traumatic memories among the people we encountered, victims of the Church's holy terror.

Under Construction

Wonder Woman Electric to the Rescue

My first close-up encounter with drag queens took place in a Tenderloin bar when I worked as an electrician with Wonder Woman Electric in the late 1970s.

An all-female collective of electricians, we did mostly residential work. But our regular commercial accounts included some of the multitude of San Francisco gay bars. Each of the bars catered to a particular subculture in the larger gay community. Lesbians had a few bars and coffee houses, but bars for gay men proliferated. The flowering of gay culture had produced bars geared toward disco queens, the leather crowd, the sweater gays, uniform wearers, beach bunnies, older gentlemen, cross dressers, fairies—as many as one could even imagine.

One day in the middle of the week I was called to a hole-in-the-wall bar in the Tenderloin. When I finally found a place to park the Wonder Woman van, it was blocks away and I had to lug my heavy tool bag through streets lined with junkies and drunks. I could see this was the bad part of town.

I found the address on Turk Street, a building with a blue and gold tile façade. The door was locked, but I saw a discreet push-button near it. I pushed it and after a moment a beautiful young man, far more femme than I, greeted me. He wore matching coral pedal pushers, a cardigan buttoned at the neck and mules with little heels. He did not look pleased to see me.

"I'm the electrician," I said hopefully. "Ok," he said, looking me over. Then his perfectly lipsticked mouth curled into a little smile. "Come with me. We've been waiting for you."

Stepping from the gray Tenderloin street into that little bar was like entering the Harry Potter magic store at Christmas. Colored lights and decorations hung from the low ceiling. Glitter littered the grungy floor.

A small-town girl who'd only lived in San Francisco for a year or so, I had just barely come out as a lesbian and had little experience with drag queens, transsexuals or transvestites, especially the big city kind. I was surprised to see a good number of patrons at the bar in the early part of the day, a mixed crowd of whites and Blacks. Some sat at the bar, some at round tables, but all looked fabulous. Most were men dressed in women's clothing. Some were dressed as over-the-top made-up drag queens, but most looked more like the gals from the office across the street, dressed in low heels and conservative skirts and blouses. I thought I overheard one of them say "fish" which was pretty funny considering I was the butchest thing in the room, wearing a flannel shirt, jeans and work boots.

The bartender looked like a tough sailor just off the boat who'd thrown on a shoulder-length blonde wig and serious makeup— several shades of eye shadow and bright red lips outlined beyond their natural borders. He worked the bar in a tasteful tailored Donna Reed housedress, popped collar and pearls, and ran the joint with cutting sarcasm delivered in a blaring voice. I felt like I was confronting the Wizard of Oz and had to keep myself from jumping back like Dorothy did when she and her three cohorts first encountered him. A person could not help being intimidated.

"Here's what we need," he directed me. "I don't want the patrons to use the bathroom without my permission. They get in there, lock the door and stay. And, honey, we all know what they do in there." I could only speculate. Drugs? Sex? Probably both. Lesbians had been known to use the bathrooms in our bars for such purposes. Where else could a couple go? And if they were quick about it and others didn't have to wait too long, we were usually forgiving.

The bartender continued, "I want to be able to push a button right here under the bar to unlock the bathroom door when someone wants to use it. Can you set that up?"

This drag queen was also a Control Queen! I looked around the room at the disapproving patrons. I was going to be responsible for limiting their bathroom privileges. I was already the villain and I hadn't even done anything yet. But I was certainly capable of installing a push button and door lock. It would be all low voltage, so I'd just have to put in a transformer and run low voltage cable. I wouldn't need to bend conduit or install junction boxes. "I can do that," I said.

I got to work, planning the job. Could I run the low voltage cable under the floor? Yes, said the bartender. There was a full basement. The beautiful young man ushered me to the basement, a dank, spider webby space with a hundred years of grime on every surface. I had to figure out where to drill up through the floor to run wires from the bar to the door lock. The job took me up and down the basement stairs and back to the van to retrieve materials and a ladder. I focused on my work and I was relieved that the patrons went back to drinking and dishing.

Finally the job was finished. I emerged from the basement coated in its crud, an anointed construction worker.

"Let's test it," I said.

Like electricians everywhere, I always got a thrill when I flipped the switch and my masterpiece (no matter how small) performed as intended. But I didn't usually have an audience. These guys understood drama far better than I and the dramatic moment of the day was all mine. I gave a nod to the bartender who pushed the button. The door buzzed open and, with a flourish, the beautiful young man entered the bathroom. It worked!

The patrons had all been watching closely and at the moment the bathroom door opened, they let out a raucous cheer. I felt as if I were making my big entrance, walking down the runway, head held high.

I bowed to their applause.

Machisma on Hayes Street

Who knows why people requested a contracting company named Wonder Woman Electric? Sometimes it was just to see women working as electricians; we were exotic. Sometimes it was because people preferred to hire women to work on their houses. We did exploit the stereotype that women are easier to work with, cleaner and neater (we made a special effort to keep our worksites clean.) Sometimes we worked for general contractors who knew our work and hired us as a subcontractor. In that case, the building owner, who might never have hired women, would be shocked to see us on the job. And sometimes the client thought they could pay us less because everyone knows women are worth less than men. Sometimes they thought our labor should be free and they didn't have to pay us at all.

Wonder Woman Electric found its clients through word of mouth mostly. I joined the collective in 1977 and immediately began to form stereotypes of clients. The working class folks who lived in the Mission and Excelsior neighborhoods of San Francisco, the ones who were scraping up the cash for the remodel or just to feed their kids, always paid their bills on time. You had the feeling that the bill got paid even if dinner was rice and beans for the next month. It was the rich clients who tried to skip out on paying. This amazed me. It didn't take long to realize that rich people as a class generally had no regard for the value or skills of tradespeople. They believed we were looking for any opportunity to rip them off. Lawyers were some of the worst. One lawyer ran a business advising rich people how to avoid paying their contractors altogether. How did they get that way? I tried to understand the psychology but finally gave up. Why fight with these people to get paid? Maybe it was best just to avoid them.

But we were listed as a licensed electrical contractor in the San Francisco phone book so we got calls from all over the city. Much of our work was residential and in poorer parts of town, but occasionally a commercial job or a job in a wealthy neighborhood would come our way.

We were delighted when Wonder Woman signed a contract to do the electrical remodel of what would be a new restaurant, the Hayes Street Grill. We knew that the owner of the new restaurant was a locally famous food critic and we looked forward to working for a female business owner. The job included an electrical service upgrade for the building, which meant digging under the sidewalk to run a rigid pipe to the power company's street box and installing a 200-amp commercial main disconnect.

Our founder, Susanne di Vincenzo, took the lead on the job. She was smart with a degree in physics. She'd been doing graduate work at Columbia when she joined with other students to shut down the university during anti-war protests in 1970. She never finished her graduate degree. Instead, she and some other former physics students learned the electrical trade in the slums of New York rerouting electricity with a Puerto Rican and Dominican squatters' movement. At that time, if you were female, the above-ground avenue toward learning the electrical trade was closed to you.

The building that would house the Hayes Street Grill was a three-story wood-frame Victorian with a steep gabled roof, a residential building that we workers would convert into a restaurant with a commercial kitchen, essentially replacing electrical, plumbing, heating and air movement systems—the guts.

Upgrading the electrical service would be the biggest job, but we would also be pulling new circuits for big kitchen equipment and a new lighting system. Much of our work would involve bending and installing electrical conduit in the unfinished basement, then drilling up through the floor to the kitchen. On jobs like this there are often no plans. The contractor designs the electrical system and then builds it. You get the manufacturer's technical requirements for each piece of equipment, then calculate the size of the wire and conduit needed.

We started with the service, the point where electricity comes into the building. Jean, Sylvia and I crouched in a three-foot high corner of the dirt crawl space where the two-inch service conduit would enter the basement from the street as Susanne gave us a code lesson on figuring the required size of a commercial electrical service. Part of this job would be disconnecting the existing service conductors and temporarily reconnecting the new wires live, a dangerous prospect. But we were glad not to have to do it while standing on a 30-foot ladder, the usual procedure when service wires are overhead. Electricians are more likely to die from falling off a ladder than from electrocution.

Normally there's no reason for the electrician to climb on top of the roof and I can't remember why I had to get up there but at one point I found myself straddling the peak. I was creeping along as carefully as I could, watching the sheet metal workers installing the big air intake and exhaust structures that ran from the kitchen to the roof on the outside of the building. Those guys had safety harnesses but I didn't. Wonder Woman Electric had no harnesses, nor any safety equipment (I used my own respirator to protect my lungs while working in attics and crawl spaces.) Instead, we should have taken job safety more seriously. In the three years I worked with the collective we had two serious fall accidents that could have been prevented if we'd had a safety program.

On the roof I tied a piece of wire around my waist and secured it around the brick chimney thinking it might break my fall. Just then the sidecutter pliers I was carrying slipped out of my tool pouch and bounced with dramatic effect off all the surfaces on the way down to the bottom of the light well forty feet below. It was suddenly easy to imagine losing my grip and tumbling to the ground. But it was a good thing I didn't fall; that wire could have cut me in half. It was just one of the stupid things I did as an electrician that could have killed me but didn't.

I think it was here that I began to understand the concept of Machisma, the female version of Machismo. Female construction workers all know that men in the trades think taking risks on the job is somehow connected to their manhood. Risky behavior is what separates the boys from the girls in the minds of the macho guys. The construction companies' owners probably loved the macho attitude, as they wouldn't have to provide personal protective equipment to their workers who thought concern for safety made you a pussy. In some ways the female version was worse—it was self-inflicted. We felt we had to be better than the men in every way, and not be afraid to take risks on the job. The five-woman crew of WWE enforced the macha credo by bucking each other up and sometimes by taunting each other when faced with a frightening task. We also helped each other in risky situations more than the men did. But I was working alone on the roof. My macha attitude melted away as I imagined myself following that hand tool down to the ground. I managed to complete my task and climb down without mishap but I was shaken.

It was our policy to write into our contracts a payment schedule based on work as it was finished. We set the main service and waited for a scheduled payment stipulated in the contract. No money came through. Why, out of all the subcontractors on the job, were we not getting paid? We never met the owner but she had no problem with our work as far as we knew. She did have partners in the enterprise and perhaps it was one of them who deigned not to pay us.

Susanne was the "forema'am" charged with dealing with the owners and she had to go through a general contractor. So when the first payment did not materialize after several weeks, Susanne pulled us off the job. We had not finished the electrical service, a technical part of the job that requires a contractor's license and knowledgeable crew. The power company, Pacific Gas and Electric, would not connect the service to their grid unless it had a green tag signifying it had been permitted, inspected and signed off by the city.

Some time later that payment came through, we figured because they learned they had to pay us in order to get the inspection and green tag. In the basement we discovered that the owners had hired an unskilled electrician to finish the interior job, apparently because they thought our bid too costly. He was likely unlicensed and had done the work without a city permit. No inspector would have let this sloppy work pass. The wiring was in conduit (a requirement for commercial work) but this guy had never learned how to bend pipe. The bends were kinked and poorly made.

We were outraged. We worried that his work would reflect on us, as one permit had been issued to us. We also worried that his poor work could cause a safety hazard in the restaurant. The purpose of the electrical code is to address safety.

We should have reported this unsafe work to the district electrical inspector. Maybe we did; I don't remember. But we certainly didn't want to give him, or anyone else, the impression that we had done the work.

As a way to register our discontent I wrote on all the conduit "WONDER WOMAN ELECTRIC NOT RESPONSIBLE FOR THIS WORK." When the general contractor saw my handiwork he was not happy but he probably figured no one would ever go down into that unfinished basement. We got our final check for the service installation and vowed never to work for these people again.

The restaurant opened in 1979 and today remains a destination for affluent opera goers. The kinked pipes might still be there. I wonder if our remonstrations were ever painted over. And I wonder about the integrity of the interior wiring in the walls. Did that unskilled electrician who didn't know how to bend pipe know how to do anything else? Did he have a license? Did he pull a permit? Was his work inspected? Did he get paid?

Dispatched

"**M**artin, take a break!"

I had been busy moving a cart full of wire spools, following the crew chief's orders. I looked up to see my coworkers sitting in a row on a platform drinking coffee. Shit. Nobody told me about coffee break. It was 10:05. Later I would learn that the 10-minute coffee break was a hard-fought clause in the union contract. To work through coffee break was to break down conditions for the entire crew. I had needed a mentor but nobody told me anything.

When I had heard that the San Francisco electricians' union, IBEW* Local 6, was looking for journeyworker hands at $17 an hour I resolved to figure out how to get in. San Francisco was experiencing a construction boom in 1980 and the union hall was empty. Local 6 had put out a call for experienced electricians. If the union could not supply skilled workers to the contractors, the contractors would have to find them, and the union was doing everything it could to maintain control of the hiring process. By that time I'd been working almost four years as a nonunion electrician with two different companies. I'd graduated from a CETA** training program in Seattle where I had learned wiring basics and how to read the electrical code like a dictionary to find out what I didn't know. I certainly felt like a journeywoman.

The deal was you put together a resume and went before the union executive board to prove you really had experience. The E board was six men sitting around a table. After a few questions about the mechanics of wiring, they approved me, but I knew they were desperate for hands. I was put on Book Five. It was all about seniority. It worked like this: Book One was local San Francisco hands who had graduated from the union apprenticeship. Book Two was journeymen from other nearby union locals. I don't know what Books Three through Five were, but the bigger your book number, the less seniority you had. Book Five was for the dregs. Last hired, first fired. You knew if you got laid off you might never get out through the union hall again.

My number came up on a foggy day in mid-August and I followed instructions to get my butt and my tools down to the union hall. I had to borrow my lover's beat-up VW bug, as I didn't have a car. Annie was one of the few dykes I knew who owned a car, and she charged us dearly for its use, but I had no choice. My toolbox was too heavy to lug onto the bus. I only had to drive from Annie's apartment on Balmy Alley in the Mission to the union hall on Fillmore Street in the Haight, but weather and mechanical issues combined to nearly defeat me. The thick summer fog lay heavily on the city, obscuring my view of the streets. It landed in tiny drops on the windshield, coalescing and running down like rain, which would have been ok had the windshield wipers not been broken. The driver's side wiper was attached to a string. I had to stick my arm out the window and operate it with my left hand while driving and shifting gears with my right. Miraculously I made it to the union hall without crashing.

The union had erected the single-story modern brick-faced hall at the southern end of Fillmore Street behind the New Mint in the Black ghetto, a neighborhood of decaying Victorians that the white brothers derided as the FillMo'. Dispatch took place in the basement of the hall. The dispatcher, a bald fat guy in a white shirt no tie, read down a list, yelling the names. When he got to mine, I approached the window and got a slip with the job information. I was to go to the symphony hall at Civic Center, a big job nearly at its end. I heard the contractor was facing penalties for going over the allotted time. Or maybe he was already paying penalties.

At the job site I checked in with the electrical crew boss whose "office" was in a basement room. The symphony hall was topped out, all the concrete had been poured, the roof and exterior walls finished. But the interior finishes, including sheetrock, were still to be done so workers' paths through the building went right through the fastest routes, around metal studs and through ghost walls yet to be finished. In the cavernous concert hall, workers from a dozen trades rushed around making finishing touches on the rough building. The job had that fresh smell of new concrete.

On my first day, the shop steward called a meeting of the crew in the basement where the contractor's big gang boxes were stored. I'd never been in one place with so many electricians. I counted 25, but they filled up this space and seemed like more. The carpenters were taking a strike vote and they wanted the support of the other trades. I didn't have to be told not to cross a picket line. But I sensed the brothers were worried about me. I was an unknown quantity and I'd worked nonunion.

My job was to do what I was told and keep my mouth shut. For $17 an hour I could do that. The crew boss instructed me to move bundles of conduit from one floor to another. Whatever. In this endeavor I had a partner, another Book Five hand, a Black guy. We were probably the only female and only African American on the whole job, certainly among the electricians. We immediately formed a bond and I felt I could count on him to stand up for me if harassed, and I let him know I would have his back.

Conduit is manufactured in diameters from a half-inch and up, cut in ten-foot lengths and bundled. I learned to pick up the bundle and, like a weightlifter, heft it up to my shoulder in one clean lift.

By the end of that day my shoulder was so sore from carrying pipe that I brought a towel to work the next day to give me a little padding. But the next day I was put on a different floor and instructed to vacuum out floor boxes. Fine with me. Near the end of the day the crew boss approached me and handed me a blue paper. Not a pink slip, a blue slip. Same thing. I was laid off. I'd never used a tool, never seen a blueprint.

Even after only two days, I was crushed. There's nothing like the bummer of getting a layoff notice even if you're looking forward to the layoff. I felt lucky in a way, as I knew the carpenters were planning to go out on strike the following day and I would never cross a picket line, so I'd probably lose the job anyway. With a layoff notice I could apply for unemployment.

Did the contractor hire a bunch of hands just to show they'd made a good faith effort to meet the contract deadline? Was I laid off because they thought they couldn't trust me to not cross the picket line, or was the crew boss doing me a favor by laying me off before the strike? There was no one to ask. I picked up my toolbox and went back to the union hall to sign the out-of-work book. Maybe there would be another short call.

*International Brotherhood of Electrical Workers
**Comprehensive Employment and Training Act

Sisters Restoring Justice

Every woman has a retribution fantasy, what she would do to her harasser or rapist. She probably won't tell you what it is but she has one, maybe many.

My group of tradeswomen activists not only imagined retribution, we planned and executed it. Perhaps corrective justice is a better choice of words.

We were an organized group of women who were trying our damnedest to break barriers to nontraditional blue-collar work. Men wanted to keep those high-paid jobs for themselves. So when one of us finally landed a job, we were subject to harassment with the aim of getting us to quit. At that time in the late seventies, sexual harassment was not yet illegal and the term was not yet in popular use. We tradeswomen used the term *gender harassment* because the harassment we experienced was usually not about sex.

We were working at integrating the construction trades, bus driving, firefighting, policing, printing, dock work—all the jobs women had been kept out of. One job classification we focused on was ferryboat deckhand. Women had won a discrimination lawsuit, a judge had signed a consent decree, and a handful of women had broken into the trade. As with construction, you had to jump both the barriers of bosses and the union.

One of our biggest challenges was isolation on the job. Once you got hired, you were usually the only female there. We tried to combat isolation by recruiting more women and by organizing support groups wherever we were.

Annie McCombs was our gal on the ferries, having made it through the union process. A militant lesbian feminist with a take no prisoners attitude, Annie was committed to increasing the number of women on the waterfront, to truly integrating the trade. After five years as a ferryboat deckhand she had gained a reputation on the docks as someone who did not tolerate abuse.

Fear of violence was based on reality. A common myth among fishers and sailors was that just letting a woman walk onto your boat was bad luck. We had met a woman fisher who had been thrown off a boat into the water by coworkers who intended to run her off for supposedly bringing bad luck to their boat.

Annie worked occasionally with another young woman, Patricia. She was Native American, a lesbian and only 18 with little work experience. One day Patricia approached Annie and told her about a guy on the job who was harassing her mercilessly. The harassment had turned violent when they worked together on the night shift. He had locked them in a bathroom they were assigned to clean and shoved her up against the wall. Only the security guard knocking on the door saved her from being raped. The guy assaulted her again the next night but she fought back and was able to break free.

Annie helped Patricia meet with her boss and the union rep, going through all the required motions. They got nowhere. The next step would be litigation, but we activists did not recommend women file individual lawsuits. That got you blacklisted and unemployed.

We resorted to direct action. Annie called a meeting and 30 women showed up. She told us about the situation and we began to strategize. How could we get this guy to back off and stop harassing our sister? We had heard about a group of women stripping a rapist naked and tying him to a pole in the middle of town. That was a great fantasy, but none of us was willing to take the chance of being arrested for assault. Whatever we did would have to be hands off. We also wanted our action to be collective, something we could all participate in. We needed to make sure this guy knew that what he was doing was wrong and that it had to stop. It would be great if the woman he had targeted could confront him directly, if we could help her feel safe enough to do that.

Jan, a tradeswoman sister, spoke up. "We need to confront this guy on our own terms in a place of our choosing, not at work," she said. "One of us should get him on a date." This seemed crazy to me. I was never any good at picking up men, but other women in the group assured me it wasn't that hard. Hadn't we been trained all our lives to do this? Jan volunteered to be the bait and we worked out an elaborate plan for her to pick him up.

She would lure him to a secluded location in Golden Gate Park where we would surround him and let Patricia confront him. I, for one, did not see how this was possible. How would we get him to the park?

Jan said she would invite him to a party at the de Young Museum and make some excuse to get him to the nearby rose garden. The rose garden is surrounded by tall hedges, perfect for hiding behind. And it's relatively dark. Our action would take place at dusk.

Word of the action got around and our planning meetings expanded to 50. Everybody wanted to be involved with this action. What militant feminist wouldn't?

We considered the possibility that the harasser might have a gun. Annie knew that some deckhands carried handguns in their seabags. Many of us practiced karate and self-defense and we engaged our martial arts experts to take command in case the perp responded violently. A woman was assigned to each limb and his head in case he reached for a gun or bolted. But unless he attacked, we were not to touch him.

Women volunteered for specific tasks: lookouts, runners, watchers from park benches. We would not leave Jan alone with the man and risk him assaulting another woman.

In the meantime, Annie drew up a map of the park with our location and she and Jan planned out the timing. We were to hide in the bushes near the trail and pop out as Jan walked by with the harasser.

I was dubious. Could we really pull this off? There were so many variables. What if he didn't go with Jan? What if he saw us in the bushes? What if the timing were hours off?

Fifty women had assembled some blocks away at a staging area in the Haight-Ashbury when a carload of country women from Mendocino County showed up. They had heard about the action through the lesbian grapevine. Now numbering more than 50, we all made our way to the rose garden.

We hid behind hedges and trees, waiting silently for maybe 20 minutes. Everybody knew the plan. I couldn't believe it when I saw Jan and the guy walking down the trail. Jan really did it! Our butch dyke sister had transformed into a fetching het woman. She wore a pink sweater wrapped casually around her shoulders.

Just as they crossed in front of us the spotter blew a whistle, the designated woman stepped out into the trail, and then all the women materialized and circled the guy. Jan melted into the crowd.

My only job was to stand in place with a mean look on my face. I can tell you this is not so easy when what one feels is exhilaration.

Our chosen spokeswoman stepped forward menacingly. She addressed the harasser. "Don't talk, just nod if you understand."

A woman was assigned to remind him to nod. He did not need

to be reminded.

"We know you have been harassing women on your job. We know where you live. We know the car you drive. If you continue to harass women we will come and get you," she said.

I could see his knees shaking. It looked to me like he had peed his pants.

Patricia stepped forward but she was not able to speak. Her partner spoke for her, naming the harassment.

Finally the crowd of angry women parted and let the man out. He was ordered to return to his car and not to look back.

Our action had succeeded. We were jubilant. A cheer went up from the 50-plus women. Then we quickly decamped to an agreed-upon location for a post-mortem and to celebrate.

As for the harasser, he was not seen around the waterfront for several months. Later, when he took a part-time job with the company, he made sure to keep his head down when passing Annie or Patricia. Soon after that he disappeared altogether.

A Sister Raped and Murdered

October 24, 1983

Pacific Heights Woman Strangled

I see the headline, then discover to my horror the woman was Sue Lawrence, a fellow electrician. Back home with Sandy gone to class and after a day full of questions from men at work I'm terrified at the prospect of my own victimization. That "nude body face down on the bed" could be mine. What if, as in some Agatha Christie plot, the murderer is going after all the female electricians in the city? Will I be next? In the shower, a most vulnerable state especially with a head full of shampoo and eyes closed, I imagine Ruth pounding on my door to be him. Panic strikes. I manage to wash shaking limbs.

****

I was not the only one terrified by Sue's murder. Other female electricians in the city had the same thought. There were so few of us since union apprenticeship programs had just recently opened their doors to women after years of pressure and lawsuits. We were in the minority. We were not welcomed. We were scorned. We already felt vulnerable as women in an all-male work environment. Now this murder had us all freaked out.

Sue's memorial was held at the Episcopal church just off Diamond Heights Blvd. We met Sue's parents and heard a minister recite a rote speech, but we learned very little more about Sue than we already knew, which was not much.

Afterward we repaired to Yet Wah, a Chinese restaurant on the upper floor of the shopping center across the street. There the women electricians of the International Brotherhood of Electrical Workers (IBEW) Local 6 gathered to celebrate the life of our sister.

We were joined by two or three tradeswomen friends from other crafts.

We had been working on construction sites that day but, as construction workers say to each other outside of work, we cleaned up pretty good. You couldn't look at us and tell that we were electricians. I wore my only "good" outfit, a sports jacket with sleeves rolled up bought at Community Thrift, the gay secondhand store on Valencia Street. Paired with black jeans and a white shirt I could go anywhere.

My roommate Sandy was a fashion plate and took this opportunity to wear a dress, a fifties number with a pencil skirt. She had a tiny waist and large hips so she had trouble finding work clothes that fit. Manufacturers didn't make work clothes for women. Away from work Sandy took refuge in skirts. She had always wanted to work in the fashion industry but couldn't find a job there. She felt she didn't fit in construction, but the money was a powerful incentive.

Others dressed in black funeral attire.

"Sharp," said Alice when she bumped into Dale, who was wearing a suit and tie. "Very *avant garde*."

Ten of us were seated around a big round table with a lazy susan in the middle for family style serving. As big plates of Gung Pao chicken and mu shu pork revolved, we collectively decompressed.

I had worked out of the Local 6 hall for a couple of years, but I had never encountered any of my sisters on the job. We were isolated and alone when at work. Our active support group of Local 6 women gathered monthly to share stories and to support each other. The sisters' gatherings helped us feel not so alone. We had been pushing for a women's caucus in our union local, a caucus with the union's endorsement.

"So I got a cease and desist letter from the union," said Sandy, whose thick Boston accent left us Westerners chuckling. "They said if we don't stop meeting they will kick us out. We are not an authorized caucus, and there's no easy way for us to get authorized."

"Are they serious?" said Joanne. "Would they really do that?"

The business manager kept a tight rein on the local. We heard those who attempted to challenge his leadership had been blacklisted, but it was hard to imagine the local disenfranchising its handful of female members. We had only just made our way in. At that time there were fewer than ten of us in the union local. We decided to keep meeting. But it was a clear message—the union was not our ally and we should not seek support there.

Sue Lawrence had entered the IBEW apprenticeship when she was only 18. She was about to graduate from the four-year program when she was raped and murdered by the stranger who broke into her parents' house.

I knew Sue only from the sisters' meetings. She didn't talk much. I didn't even remember having a conversation with her.

"She was weird," said Dale. "A newspaper reporter called and asked about Sue. I didn't know what to say. I think she was suffering from manic depression. But, hey, we all know you have to be a little bit crazy to go into the trades as a woman."

Nods around the table. We all felt a little bit crazy.

"I know she struggled during her apprenticeship," said Jan. "You know she started right out of high school. That's rough. Younger women get more harassment. But she made it through and she was just about to turn out as a journeywoman."

"The last project she worked on was that big housing complex at the ocean where Playland at the Beach used to be," said Dolores.

"She was the only woman working there."

"I think she was struggling with her sexuality," said Alice.

Sue was an enigma to all of us. Had any of us been there to support her? Maybe not to the extent we should have been.

Sue lived with her parents in the house she had grown up in on Green Street. I had driven by it just to see where she came from. It was a rich part of town that none of us frequented. Her parents had some money. Maybe Sue hadn't fit into the box prepared for her. She was an unlikely electrician, but I knew several of them—women whose parents were doctors and who rebelled against parental expectations by going into construction.

"Can I be honest," said Lynn. "Since Sue was murdered I haven't slept well. I'm scared. Was Sue attacked because she was an electrician? Are we at risk of being attacked?"

We looked at each other. I hadn't slept well either. We didn't know anything about Sue's killer. What was his motive?

Jennifer told us how she had been attacked and raped in her own house the year before. Sue's death had been hard on her. The only female on her job, she couldn't shake the thought that her coworkers might be abusers and rapists. She had stayed off the job and was terrified to go back to work where she felt profoundly unsafe. She confessed that she didn't know how much longer she could stay in the apprenticeship.

"Maybe I have PTSD or something," she said. "Whenever I think about going back to work I get the cold sweats. I'm starting to think I just can't go back."

Tradeswomen can't get together without talking about discrimination and harassment we experience on the job. No one else really understands or wants to listen to our complaints.

Pat, who had started in one of the first apprenticeship classes of Local 6 women in 1978, complained about being dyke baited.

"One of the guys called me a bulldagger the other day," she bellowed. Pat had a mouth on her. Maybe that's how she survived.

Pat was married to a man and they had two young children. I had seen a picture of her at her graduation from the apprenticeship. She was standing next to her tuxedoed husband and dressed in a fancy gown made of filmy blue material like women might have worn to any other graduation ceremony. Even in that gown Pat looked like the butchest bull dyke we knew. She kept her hair short and had a stocky body. On the job in her work clothes and tool belt Pat radiated authority. How sad to have to put up with dyke baiting when you're not even a dyke!

"Pat should officially be an honorary dyke," I said. "She gets dyke baited just like us lesbians, maybe even more."

And we all agreed. Dale stood and, pretending to wield a magic sword, touched Pat on both shoulders and declared, "Pat, I now dub you an honorary dyke. Your ID card will be mailed to you."

And it was then that I truly understood that dyke baiting was not as much about lesbians as it was about ensuring that we all meet certain stereotypes of what men think women should look and act like. Dyke baiting on the job affected all of us, gay and straight.

The conversation turned to tradeswomen organizing. We had been making an effort to hire childcare for our meetings and conferences but it was a struggle. We had no budget so we resorted to passing the hat to hire a childcare worker. The dearth of childcare meant that some of our parent members had to bring their kids to meetings or stay home. The only woman at the table with kids, Pat supported a childcare initiative.

"But you've got a husband," said Alice. "Why can't he stay with the kids."

"Yeah I'm married, but you've got a partner too," countered Pat. "This is just discrimination against mothers. Do you want us in the group or not?"

Samantha, sitting across the table, sent me a look. We had been flirting for weeks. She was so damn cute, curly dark hair framing a round face, a small woman with a muscled frame. We had been lifting weights together at the Women's Training Center on Market Street.

It was a period in my life when attractions proliferated and sometimes the attraction could not be ignored. Sam's look required follow up. She politely excused herself from the table and I waited a moment before heading in the direction of the women's room.

The bathroom had two stalls. Sam entered the one nearest the wall. I was close behind, gliding in and locking the door. Smiling, I caressed her firm delts. I knew how much she could bench. She was so hot. I gently pressed her back up against the door and lowered my head slightly. The kiss—long and soft—weakened my knees.

Others crowded into the bathroom.

"Hey, can I have some of that too," called Dale, looking under the door at our four feet.

Busted!

We walked out with sheepish grins to a line of sister construction workers waiting for the stall.

"Get a room," someone yelled.

They were taunting us but they were all laughing. And then we were laughing too, a practiced survival tactic.

****

October 27, 1983

Sue's memorial service and dinner with the women electricians afterward inspires me to see these women as my sisters in struggle. I feel our collective rage and hurt and vulnerability. When I tell them I imagine a plot against women electricians, all admit the same horrible fantasy. Jennifer who survived being raped and strangled in her own house last year is hardest hit but others tell of their terror at staying alone at home.

****

Though I conflate these events in my mind, it wouldn't be until six years later that we would witness a mass killing of women who deigned to study what had been "men's work." On December 6, 1989, Marc Lépine entered a mechanical engineering class at the École Polytechnique in Montreal and separated the women, telling the men to leave the room. He said he was "fighting feminism" and opened fire. He shot at all nine women in the room, killing six. He then moved through corridors, the cafeteria, and another classroom, targeting women. He slaughtered eight more before turning the gun on himself.

That guy had a motive.

Work Boots Step Out of the Closet

"Come on you can tell me," says Bobby. "Are you gay?"

Bobby is a machinist who usually works in the machine shop but today he is helping me change light fixtures in the warehouse at the corporation yard. I'm the only electrician and sometimes I need a helper. There was no laborer available and I am up on a 16-foot ladder.

The song by the Police, *Every Breath You Take*, is playing on the boombox he carries around with him.

"This sounds like a song about stalking," I say. "It's a threat."

"Hmm, I never thought about it that way," he says, "but I guess you're right."

I've been at the San Francisco Water Department for a few months and I'm getting along all right. Especially considering I'm the only tradeswoman there except for Amy, the only female plumber. Amy is out digging up the streets every day and so I rarely see her. Sometimes we convene a two-woman support group in the women's restroom and it's good to know she's there.

I think about how to answer Bobby. It kind of annoys me that he would just ask me like that. But on the other hand I appreciate his directness. I like Bobby and he's as close to a friend as I have among the men, but I know if I give him any information about my private life it will be all over the yard within 24 hours. Do I want all the guys in all the shops to know?

"That's none of your business," I reply.

Yeah, I'm a lesbian and my lover is Del, who works at Park and Rec. We were both female firsts—she the first carpenter and I the first electrician to work for the city of San Francisco. Being the first is always a burden. You are aware that you set the stereotype for all the women who come after you. You feel the whole of womankind rests on your shoulders. You know you can't make mistakes but of course you do, and then you imagine all of womankind suffers.

Del is five foot two and slender but you don't see her as small. Her wiry gray hair gives her a couple more inches of height. She's got broad shoulders and large hands. And she gets power from her low voice; she sings tenor with a gay chorus, the Vocal Minority.

Del and I don't live together but I spend a lot of time at her apartment on Potrero Hill with its sweeping view of the bay and downtown. At my place in Bernal Heights I have a roommate, Sandy, another electrician. She's messy and has a lot of stuff and a cokehead girlfriend I don't like. So I often stay with Del. Truth is I can't stay away. I'm mad for her.

Since I got into the trades, my lovers have been tradeswomen. I can't resist a woman with a toolbelt. The first woman I fell in love with was a carpenter. They say you either fall in love with her or you want to be her. For me it was both.

I watch my lover Nancy build a house. She wears dirty blue jeans and scuffed work boots. Sweat stains mushroom on her T-shirt, which reads Sisterhood is Powerful, *under a women's symbol with a fist in its center. Sweat drips from her nose and rolls down the side of her face. Her sun-bleached curly hair sticks out from under her hardhat.*

Around her hips hangs the heavy leather carpenter's belt. It has a metal ring for the hammer and slots for the tape measure and various other tools, and pouches for the nails of different sizes. A two-inch wide leather belt holds it around her ample hips. It's helped by wide suspenders. She grabs a handful of nails and holds them with all the heads lined up in one direction, flips them down and pounds them into the wood with great efficiency. Tanned arms bulge as she sinks nail after nail into the sill plate. She is focused and fast, the epitome of strength and ease. When she takes a break, she rolls a cigarette and lights it with a match put to her boot. She sucks in the smoke with obvious pleasure and even though I'm super allergic to smoke and it will set me off coughing, that is the sexiest thing I've ever seen. How could a gal not fall in love with this image of power, strength, purpose.

I was smitten and I've been smitten by tradeswomen ever since. And they are the only ones who really understand what I go through at work. A person's got to have a partner she can whine to when she gets home.

Lately it's Del who's been having trouble at work. Dick, her boss at the carpentry shop, doesn't like women or queers. He does everything he can to make her work life difficult. If it weren't for Dick, Del would get along just fine. She loves the work, not the harassment. She once overhead him call her a dyke. That's a word we lesbians have reclaimed and embraced but he meant it in the old-fashioned derogatory way.

Negotiating homophobia and sexism at work is a balancing act for us. You just know that the boss will use any excuse to lay you off. Del knows this too, that we women must always keep our cool in these situations, but sometimes she can't help herself. She just loses her temper and then even she doesn't know what she might do.

One time she held off an attacker with a hand saw. If you swing it at waist level, they can't reach you. She swung the saw in a fit of rage, acting without thinking. In that case rage saved her ass, but mostly when this happens she leaves the confrontation feeling embarrassed that she could not control her emotions. She tells me I'm much better at not losing my cool and she ascribes her rage to her hot Italian blood.

I first met Del at a tradeswomen confab when I was working with the Wonder Woman Electric collective in 1978, but we didn't get together as lovers until 1982 while we were organizing the first national tradeswomen conference that took place in Oakland the next year. We had both been working construction downtown before starting to work for the city of San Francisco.

"I lost my temper today and now I might lose my job," Del told me one evening when I got over to her place after work.

By that time she was remorseful. "Why do I always lose my temper? How do you manage to stay so cool?"

I think the answer lays in the ways we learned to respond to stress and abuse when we were growing up. She was a caretaker type and I was oblivious. Del says she always felt like she had antennae, that she was super aware of her surroundings. I, on the other hand, would put on virtual blinders and just continue pretending nothing was going on. This method of avoiding conflict has served me well in the trades. I pretend not to see and often I really don't.

Soon after we got together I accompanied her to visit her family in Chicago. Right away I felt at home. They are huggers, and loud talkers, people who like to cook and eat big family meals and who live in their basements, never using the living room upstairs where couches are covered with plastic. Her mother is part of a big Italian clan—all sisters except for one brother who is treated like a king but drowned out by loud women.

"Here's what happened," she said. "I wanted to get my paycheck earlier in the day than Dick wanted to give it out. I had an appointment and was leaving at noon. He was being totally obnoxious about it and I got really mad at him. I said 'fuck it' and walked out without the paycheck. Now he's trying to fire me for swearing at him. I wasn't swearing at him, it was a general fuck-it. Anyway, just an excuse to fire me."

"I'm scared," she admitted.

"What are you gonna do now?" I asked, concerned.

"I don't have a plan except to wait to see what he does next. Maybe it won't go anywhere."

A few days later Dick upped the ante. He set up a kangaroo court with his supervisors and friends in the yard who sat Del down and questioned her. She had no representation or support. It was just a set up.

That's when Del went above the boss's head. We knew that the director of Park and Rec was an out gay man. Tom had gained a reputation as a respected department head who gave a shit about workers. He was also a player in the gay South of Market scene who (we heard) had tattoos all over his body. He always wore long-sleeved shirts at work.

"Tom was absolutely great when I told him the story and showed him the daily journal I'd kept about the harassment," she said to me. Soon after that Dick was fired.

Our gay ally had saved Del's job, but what would have happened had he not been there?

"Are you out on the job," she asked me later.

"Well...no, I admitted. "It's none of their business."

Del is a proponent of coming out at work. She says it's better to give the guys the information so they will just stop gossiping about you. For women it might actually be a plus to be out. It's a signal that you're not interested in them romantically and you never will be, a good way to stop come-ons. Telling them you're married with five kids works too.

At the tradeswomen conference she gave a workshop to help gay women come out.

"If we all come out we won't be alone," she says. "We'll be supporting our lesbian sisters."

She quoted Harvey Milk: "Every gay person must come out. As difficult as it is, you must tell your immediate family. You must tell your relatives. You must tell your friends if indeed they are your friends. You must tell the people you work with. You must tell the people in the stores you shop in. Once they realize that we are indeed their children, that we are indeed everywhere, every myth, every lie, every innuendo will be destroyed once and all. And once you do, you will feel so much better."

Del was pissed when I confessed I wasn't out on the job. "What!" she exclaimed. "You're still in the closet at work! Don't you see why it's important for us all to be out? How can you leave me hanging out there on a limb? I almost lost my job!"

She had a good point—several good points. I thought about why I'd stayed closeted. It was easier. I didn't want to risk the wrath and disdain of my co-workers. They weren't really interested in my private life and I couldn't care less about theirs. It was hard enough just being the only female on the job. You imagine the worst thing that could happen. They wouldn't physically attack me. But they could refuse to work with me just as one white guy in the machine shop had refused to work with a Black guy. They could refuse to talk to me, a trick men used on women all the time to get them to quit. They could fire me. I'd been hired on as a temporary worker with no employment rights. I wasn't safe.

But I promised my lover I would come out.

My electric "shop" was a windowless closet next to the machine shop office where my boss, Manuel, and a secretary worked. They were always trying to get me to fill in when she was out sick, which happened with regularity. I had made the mistake of answering truthfully when they'd asked if I could type. I'd refused and I hadn't relented even when Bud, the auto shop boss cried crocodile tears as he tried to type with hands missing several of their fingers. Somehow the guy was still able to work on trucks. But that was men's work.

One day Manuel made a reference to my husband. That was my opening. I hadn't had to wait long.

"I don't have a husband," I said. "I'm gay."

When you come out to them, men are either totally shocked or they tell you they knew all along. Manuel was shocked, but he recovered quickly.

I didn't have to tell anyone else. Word got around the yard. I heard one of the machinists, a religious nut, had moved me into the hated category. But he was someone I could avoid.

Bobby was cool. "I knew it," he said.

How Do You Say Goodbye?

Joe is talking about death. "I don't know how to say goodbye," he says.

I look up from the electrical outlet I'm installing, bending a piece of half-inch pipe as he continues.

"Say you have a good friend who's dying," he says. "How do you say goodbye?"

I'm suspicious. These men think that because I'm female I'll mother them. I'll listen to their problems. Let them cry on my shoulder. Tell them everything's alright. I resent the emotional drain on me. What do I get in return? They wouldn't listen to my problems, and I wouldn't trust their intuition anyhow. Besides, I wouldn't risk making myself vulnerable to them. My usual strategy is to remain emotionally distant. Change the subject. Work, the weather, anything but intimate details. But Joe never talks like this. I'm curious.

"Do you have a friend who's dying?" I wonder.

"No, no, no." He lights a cigarette and runs a hand through gray wavy hair. "That was just an example. It's hard to say goodbye even when you hate the bastard and never want to see him again. How would you do it?"

I fit the pipe against the wall. Perfect. "I suppose I would just say goodbye. This wall isn't concrete, this is sheetrock. How am I gonna anchor anything to this? I didn't bring toggle bolts." I pound the wall nervously, vigorously listening for studs.

"Well, what do you think happens when you die? Do you believe in an afterlife? I think, when you die, you die. The human body is like a machine. It just wears out and that's that."

I find a stud, position the pipe, set my level on it, then screw in a strap which holds it in place. "That's an appropriate point of view for a stationary engineer. Just keep throwing WD40 at it until it wears out."

But he's serious. "That's another thing I never understood, the Catholic hell. I've had a running battle with hell for years. Are you religious?"

"Naw." I search through my toolbox for channel locks to tighten the compression connectors. "Seems to me just the fact that there are so many religions in the world and most of them claim to be the only true one is an overwhelming contradiction. Besides, if I were to choose a religion, the first question I'd ask is whether it's sexist. That wouldn't leave me with a lot of choices."

The door opens and the roar of the pump station engulfs the office. Jesus, one of Joe's corps of engineers steps in, in mock military fashion. He was once a transexual, presenting as female, taking hormones and planning gender reassignment surgery. But, since hospitalization after a bad traffic accident, he's gone back to being a man. Jesus has shown me pictures of himself as a woman. Beautiful then, he has since become rather paunchy, and I find it difficult to visualize him as female. I can imagine his thick, black, curly hair in a shoulder-length style. I think his movements could be convincingly female. He's short enough to pass. But how, I wonder, did he manage to conceal his heavy beard and the inevitable five o'clock shadow.

Jesus wants to know what kind of pizza we want for lunch. After weeks of pestering, Joe is apparently buying. Jesus hates anchovies, Joe hates onions. I say I want onions *and* anchovies.

Joe hands money to Jesus and hunkers over his desk, lighting another cigarette and puffing intently. "I can't wait till I can retire from this place. I'll have twenty years this year."

"How old are you?" I push the steel fish tape through the pipe to the junction box at its end.

"Fifty-two in August."

He looks 65, I think. A handsome man whose skin has aged, whose hands and jowls are puffy from too much drink. I'm certain now that Joe is drunk, and I'm alarmed. His reputation as an alcoholic is well-known, and he makes no secret of it, but I know he's been sober for a year. And, while he's made light of it, I know that staying on the wagon must have been really tough.

"When in our lives do they let us know what life is about?" he asks the wall thoughtfully. "When do we find out what we're supposed to do with our lives? Here I am over 50 and I still don't know what I'm doing here. What do you think the point is?"

I hook wires to the end of the fish tape and marvel at being a participant in this conversation. Must I really try to explain the meaning of life to this man?

"Well, I can't say I know the answer to that. I think we all start off just trying to survive," I offer.

"You kids can't understand," he puffs. "I can't explain it to my kids, either. You never consider what it's like to get old."

I pull the fish tape back through the pipe, careful not to strip the wires' plastic insulation. "Joe, you underestimate me. I'm not a kid. At 35, some people might even consider me middle-aged."

As I'm hooking up the wires, Jesus signals that the pizza has arrived. We walk through the plant past massive motors and pumps whose function is to supply water to the city of San Francisco. Even with the coffee room door shut, their constant humming provides background noise. Jesus has set the table and pulled up three chairs.

"Just like a Mexican. Where's my change?" Joe admonishes. Jesus is an American citizen but grew up in Mexico and speaks with a heavy accent. Joe turns to me. "I can say that to him 'cause I'm Mexican too."

I don't believe him. "Where'd you get those blue eyes, Joe."

"My father was Polish. He went to Mexico to work in the mines, met my mother, and they moved to New York. He was a no-good bastard, but I loved my old man."

Jesus serves the pizza, opens cans of soda. The phone rings and he goes to answer it in the office.

"I really care about people," Joe chews and ruminates, "but what do I get. They stick me out here and give me crazies like that faggot spic to work with." He gestures in Jesus's direction.

Joe's display of prejudice surprises me. He is a well-liked boss, and I always thought him equally enthusiastic about his employees. Besides, I know Jesus to be a conscientious worker, and certainly more sensitive than any other man I work with. Having been both a man and a woman in the trades has provided him with a unique perspective. He's earned my loyalty.

As I debate how to raise the issue of discrimination, Joe talks on. "I would like to help people, but they would probably tell me to go to hell. What would you say if I tried to help you?"

"You have helped me, Joe. You always answer my questions without bullshitting me."

"That's work," he says. "I'm not talking about work. I'm talking about life. I could help you. For example, I'd like to tell you to stop wearing men's clothes."

I take a bite of pizza and think how best to be diplomatic. "Go to hell, Joe."

"You see, that's what I thought you'd say. There's something else. How would you feel if I told you I want to kiss you?"

I'm furiously running my hand through my hair, willing myself (unsuccessfully) not to blush, and simultaneously pushing my chair away from him. Where the hell is Jesus? Joe is trying to make himself understood. He waves his hands, shakes his head. "Now don't get me wrong," he blunders. "Do you know what I'm trying to say?"

"Yeah, I know." I try to affect calm. "You're saying that sometimes our emotions aren't appropriate to the situation."

"Yes, yes, that's right." He looks expectant.

"Well, Joe, I would say this is one of these situations where emotions ought to be suppressed."

Jesus returns, Joe is requested to respond to an emergency breakdown. I return to my work, shaken and angry at Joe for verbalizing his feelings. He probably won't remember this conversation, but I won't forget it, and our comfortable relationship will change.

As I pass his desk, I see a note, written apparently to himself. It says, "I don't know how to say goodbye."

Why Would You Want to Be a Woman?

"I don't get it," I said. "Why would you want to be a woman? We are discriminated against. The men we work with hate us. We get paid less. Why choose that?"

Jesus thought for a moment. "When I get in the shower and look down at my penis, I hate it. I feel like it shouldn't be there."

We were standing out in the corporation yard, away from our coworkers in the shops.

Jesus and I had worked together at the San Francisco Water Department for a couple of years and I was glad we'd become close enough for me to ask such a personal question. I was starting to get it.

But I was skeptical. "Jesus, you grew up with male privilege. How do you know what it will be like?"

"I know because I've already lived as a woman," he said. "For three years."

Jesus is a stationary engineer. His job is to maintain the pump stations for the San Francisco Water Department. I'm the electrician whose job is to maintain the electrical components of the system. I work out of a corporation yard in the industrial southeast part of the city. Each of us works alone but we often encounter each other out in the field at the pump stations. In a world of macho plumbers and engineers we gravitate toward each other, more because we are different than because we are the same. We are both outcasts and we both must live within the dominant paradigm: a sexist and racist work culture with coworkers who believe we don't belong there. It's their territory.

It's 1983. I'm a temporary worker with no benefits. I could be fired at any time with no recourse. I feel like I have to prove myself every day. I'm not out of the closet at work and I worry that this information might lead to a layoff.

The men think they can talk to me about Jesus. I wonder if they talk to him about me, but I think he is even more of an outsider than I am, transgender and Mexican. I'm a white lesbian and usually the only female. When you're a double or triple minority you can never be sure why you are targeted for harassment.

"Is he gay?" they ask me. And I must try to explain transgender to these dickheads.

I know Jesus endures discrimination and harassment. The men he works with simply refuse to talk to him. They pretend he's not there. I know from experience that this form of harassment takes a toll. It's a way to get you to leave and it often works.

Despite all this Jesus appears to be the happiest person in the yard. He's always singing or humming to himself and he has cemented a stereotype in my mind of Mexicans as people who smile through adversity. Yeah, I know that's politically incorrect. I know that not all Mexicans are happy. Still, my brain forms stereotypes without my permission and I figure it's best to acknowledge it, at least to myself. Jesus sets a good example for me. I tend to react to sexism and homophobia with anger. I can't express it and so I walk around with the anger inside. And I take it home with me.

One day I'm assigned to work at the Lake Merced pump station in the southwest part of the city. That's where the huge water supply pipes come in from the city's Hetch Hetchy reservoir in the Sierra Nevada mountains. The pump motors here are 100 HP and they run on 4,600 volts. (The highest voltage supplied to our homes is 220 volts.) The switchgear supplying the motors hums in a giant metal cabinet.

I'm the only electrician and it's my job to maintain this equipment. But I've never been trained on high voltage. The union didn't let women into its apprenticeship program and so I've learned the basics in a federal job training program and from experience. I easily passed the civil service test for electrician but I've never worked on more than 480-volt systems.

When the chief engineer orders me to diagnose a problem in the switchgear, I do my best to appear competent. In troubleshooting, the first step is to test. I pull out my trusty tester, a little black box with two wire leads and touch the leads to the live switchgear.

Electricians reading this will know what happens next—my tester is only rated for 1,000 volts.

With an ear-splitting bang the tester blows up and I'm thrown backward, landing on my butt on the concrete floor.

Jesus, the engineer on duty, rushes over, looking alarmed. "Are you ok?" he asks.

"I'm ok I'm ok," I say. It's the first thing we always say after a disaster, even if not true. The loud blast affected my hearing. It sounds like we're underwater.

I could have been killed. I could have been killed. Joe, the chief engineer, knows this. He has seen the explosion and he makes a quick exit, better to not be part of this.

The first emotion I register is embarrassment. I should have used the pole tester, rated for this purpose, but it's a tool I'd never used before. I know I represent my gender to these men and my worth and work will determine their stereotypical view of women in their workplace. Their ideas of working with women will be based on me, until other females come along. My huge blunder will make all women look bad.

I'm embarrassed and I'm shaken, one minute regretting my mistake and the next thinking I could be dead. *I could be dead. Stupid stupid stupid.*

Jesus leads me into the chief engineer's office where I try to recover, crouching in a corner on the floor, hugging my knees to alleviate the shaking. *I could be dead. I could be dead.* Jesus stays with me for moral support. And that's when he tells me his story.

He grew up in Mexico City where he learned the trade of stationary engineer, maintaining the systems in big buildings. Then he migrated to San Francisco, became a US citizen and got a job working as an engineer for another city department. That's when he first decided to transition from male to female. He was living as a female, taking hormones and contemplating surgery when he was in a serious car accident. After time in the hospital he decided to go back to being male. That was several years earlier. In his present job he has always been male, but word got around and his coworkers know he once presented as female.

But he's not happy as male. This is not who he really is. He's thinking again about transitioning. He's saving money for the operation and figures it will cost about $10,000.

"I want to tell you something I've never told anyone at work," I say. "I'm gay." And with that a sense of relief fills me. I'm no longer alone here.

Jesus nods. "I thought so," he says, "but thanks for telling me."

This admission makes me feel I can ask him anything without offending him.

"So are you attracted to men or women? If you transition will you be a lesbian?"

"I'm attracted to women," he says. "Gender is different from sexual attraction."

"I know," I say. "I don't want to be a man, but I sure would like some of that male privilege."

Jesus tells me he has gone to meetings of trans groups in the city, but he never feels like he belongs anywhere. He has no community.

To me this is tragic. I depend on my lesbian and tradeswomen communities to survive as an outsider.

"What was it like for you being a woman in the trades?" I ask.

"They assume a man knows everything," he says. "That's challenging, because of course we don't. But we have to act like we do. It can lead to unsafe behavior. We're all supposed to be cowboys.

"They assume a woman knows nothing. That has its own drawbacks. They refuse to pass on knowledge. They take your tools away and don't want to let you do anything."

The last thing I want to be is a woman who knows nothing. Nor do I want to out macho the boys, to act like I know something when I don't. Doing that has nearly killed me.

Jesus would never say it. He's too polite and gentlemanly. But I understand his point—don't act like a dick.

Call Her by Her Name

Al and I first met when I walked into the open door at Summit pump station. He was kneeling on the concrete floor painting one of the pump motors that supply water to the city of San Francisco. When he saw my figure standing in the doorway he jumped back, like I was there to assault him. That gave me a little jolt of power—that a man might be startled by me. *Yeah*, I thought to myself, *I'm a big strong woman and men flinch at the sight of my form.* But there was a safety issue. The pump stations are situated in remote parts of the city. And I wasn't supposed to be there. Or, in reality, no one knew where I was at any particular moment. As the one electrician responsible for all the stations, I kept my own schedule, responding sometimes to complaints or work orders and sometimes just checking to make sure the electrical equipment was working.

"Hey," he said, squinting at me in the sun glaring through the open door. "Who are you?"

"I'm the electrician. Who are you?" I answered. But I knew he was a stationary engineer. Painting motors is part of their job.

The corps of engineers worked out of the Lake Merced pump station where they reported to the chief engineer, Joe. I thought I'd met all of them at one or another pump station. But Al was a retiree just filling in for a coworker who was in rehab. I figured he was about three decades older than me, a small redhead still with a good bit of hair left. He reminded me of a leprechaun—little and cute. We liked each other immediately and over the course of a few months we became friends. Not the kind of friends who see each other outside of work. But we would share personal information that we might not share with others.

There was one other engineer I was tight with, Jesus, and he would sometimes meet up with me and Al at lunch break. Jesus was transitioning from male to female and had been taking hormones for a few months. He had saved up enough money for the operation and was in the process of scheduling it. Al told me Jesus had announced to their fellow engineers that he now wanted to be called Rosa.

"How did they react?" I asked, thinking that must have taken some courage.

"They looked at their hands and didn't say anything," he said. "Just some snickering." Knowing that he was planning to transition, his coworkers had ignored Jesus and refused to talk to him. Now that he was Rosa, the treatment would be no different.

Jesus told me he had known he was really female from the time he was a child in Mexico. A generally happy person with a positive attitude, Rosa was positively delighted to finally be female, to be herself. I thought she radiated serenity.

I wish I could say the transition was seamless for me, that I found it easy to switch from Jesus to Rosa, but I found it difficult. I had gotten to know this person as Jesus and now it was like I was having to start all over again. The pronoun thing confounded me. Back in the day we feminists had pushed to rid the English language of male and female pronouns, but the idea never took hold. I dearly wished for those genderless pronouns whenever I screwed up, but Rosa was forgiving.

I was suspicious of most of the men at work. Let's just say they didn't welcome me, the lone female, into the fold. I tried to give them as little information about myself as possible, assuming it would be used against me. I knew that I could not be friends with these men. But I had begun to feel differently about Al and Jesus.

I learned that Al was married to a French woman, that they had no children. I learned that he had been around the world as a seaman. Like many of the engineers, Al had learned his trade in the Merchant Marines. I knew some things about the Merchant Marines—that the celebrated San Francisco Communist Bill Bailey had been one and that he was not the only commie. I knew that the mariners had performed a vital service in World War II, risking their lives to supply materiel to the fronts. I knew that, while they weren't part of the military, the merchant navy had suffered a higher casualty rate than any branch of the military. Their boats were always being torpedoed. Then, after the war, they were attacked and denied any benefits because they were all branded as Communists, which of course most of them were not. They were just civilian patriots willing to risk their lives to protect the lives of others.

I knew enough to gain some trust with Al before asking but I had to ask, "Were you a Communist?"

All I got was a wry smile, enough to let me know I should stop asking questions.

But that was enough for me. I call myself a communist with a small c, more of a new leftist. I'm always delighted to meet up with the old commies, for whom I have great regard. They don't always want to admit past affiliations. Most of the Reds were disheartened by knowledge of Stalin's murderous legacy. Many were hounded for years by Hoover's FBI. Jobs were lost and lives ruined.

Now it was 1985, the depths of Reaganism, which made all of us minorities jumpy and skittish and gave our detractors permission to be openly hostile. The AIDS epidemic was ravaging San Francisco's gay men's community while Reagan refused to even acknowledge the disease. Women—feminists--had come under attack along with anyone who didn't fit into the back-to-the-fifties scenario. Immigrants, transgender people and Communists too. Maybe that's why the three of us gathered, just to know we weren't alone.

Jesus, now Rosa, had begun presenting as female, letting her hair grow and wearing women's clothes. But she didn't really look that different than before. We all wore work clothes. My work outfit consisted of boots, canvas work pants, a T-shirt with a flannel shirt over the top, and when it was cold a wool-lined vest or jean jacket. A hard hat was not required on this maintenance job and I didn't have to wear a tool belt. I carried my hand tools in a canvas tool bag. And I drove a truck painted Water Department colors, Kelly green and white, in which I carried wire, pipe, benders and all the other tools and material I might need. Rosa, when dressed in work clothes, looked like me.

Rosa was the first transgender person I got close to, but I was not completely naïve. Ire had been raised in the tradeswomen community when we learned of a transgender female carpenter in our midst. She had transitioned after working as an already skilled male carpenter. She was getting work while we were frozen out because we were women. The contractor got to count her as an affirmative action hire. It didn't seem fair. Then there was a continuing dustup in the lesbian community about a transgender sound engineer who worked for Olivia Records, the women's music company. She had been trained while still male. We women wanted to do everything ourselves, but we didn't have the skills because we couldn't access the training. It's possible that when the engineer, Sandy Stone, was hired, there *were* no other female sound engineers. Some lesbians were quick to attack the individual, but most of us understood that our real enemy was the system that discriminated against women.

At lunch one day Al told us some war stories. He said he had survived a torpedo attack where some seamen had died. I tried to imagine his life on those ships. I'd heard the gay historian Allan Bérubé's lecture and slide show about sailors and soldiers during the war. They were all having sex with each other, especially the sailors. I knew Al wasn't gay but I suspected he'd participated in gay sex.

I had allowed myself to relax a little with Al and Jesus. I came out to them. We talked politics. We all hated Reagan. I had started to feel comfortable with these guys.

Then one day while Al and I worked together he confessed that his wife no longer wanted to have sex with him and he was super horny. Did I want to have sex with him? It wasn't as if men at work had not come on to me before. This was the typical way they did it; they would complain about their wives and that would be the opening. But I was shocked to hear this from my friend Al. I'd been solidly in the friend category I thought. Suddenly I was in the gal toy category. Or was it the whore category? Weird.

I said, "Al you know I'm gay. I'm not attracted to men." Which wasn't entirely true. I'd lived much of my life as a practicing heterosexual.

"Well, maybe you have friends who might want to have sex with me," he said. And for a moment I actually considered the question. I definitely had horny friends. But who might want to have sex with Al? What would his personal ad look like? "65-year-old leprechaun seeks sex with any female. Age not important. Nothing else important."

Then I was grossed out thinking my friend Al wanted me to

pimp out my women friends. Then I was disappointed that our friendship was not what I had thought it was.

"So you only have sex with women?" Al asked.

"Well yeah. That's what being a lesbian means. Maybe I'm not as sexually fluid as you. I know what y'all did on those ships."

No response except that wry smile again.

That interaction changed my relationship with Al, but he may not have even noticed. Like many men he lacked a certain amount of sensitivity. On the other hand, his size and his politics—his minority status in the world of men—engendered more empathy than most.

So now I started thinking Al was like all the other guys. I stopped feeling so safe around him. Not that he might attack me. No, I was pretty sure I could take him in a fight. I was bigger and I practiced karate. It was more that he didn't value me, didn't see who I really was, and so might not understand the need for discretion. I did know that just because someone is or was a Communist does not mean they are not sexist as hell.

For a while I didn't cross paths with Rosa. I still saw Al out in the field and he would fill me in on Rosa's transition. The surgery had gone well and Rosa was back at work. She was happy, even as her coworkers continued to give her the cold shoulder.

"I'm having trouble re-learning Jesus's name," I confessed. "I'm just not good at it. I get all confused with the pronouns and I keep saying him instead of her."

This time Al's response was sharp and I realized he must be doing his best to protect Rosa from harassment by the other engineers.

"She is Rosa now," he said, "and you've got to call her by her name."

It was an admonishment and I took it seriously. Al was worldly wise and maybe had known other transgender people. He knew how to be an ally. Could I really be learning something from this old white guy?

I guess everybody's got something to teach.

What Old Tradeswomen Talk About

My friend Marg was building a coffin for her friend Bob. Marg was happy and excited that she could give back in this way, being a carpenter. But her project plans had to take into account her disability, a persistent back pain that had put an end to her career as a building inspector and that she now spends her life managing.

When we get together Marg and I often collaborate on inventions and engineer projects that never get built. But now she was actually completing one of them.

The funeral home had given Marg the dimensions of the concrete box that the coffin would have to fit into, with the admonition that another coffin builder had exceeded the dimensions and at the burial the coffin had not fit.

At lunch with our retired carpenter friend Pat, Marg described her plan—a rectangular box rather than the typical hexagonal coffin shape. She used one four-by-eight sheet of plywood ripped in half lengthwise for the sides and ends. Another ripped sheet made the bottom and top. She made the handles with rope.

"I had the lumberyard rip the ply for me, to save my back," said Marg. "I can still use a Skilsaw to crosscut short lengths but I don't do ripping anymore."

She screwed a ledger around the inside of the box so the bottom could just be dropped in and sit on the ledger. I'm an electrician, not a skilled carpenter, so I was proud of myself for knowing that a ledger is the ribbon of wood attached to the framing of a wall that the floor hangs on. I could totally visualize it.

"What size plywood are you using?" asked Pat.

"Half-inch," said Marg.

"Cross bracing?" asked Pat.

"Well, no," said Marg. "I don't think it needs it. I used structural plywood. Anyway, the coffin is now at the funeral home."

Pat and I looked at each other and each knew what the other was thinking. I imagined the bottom piece of plywood bending with the weight of Bob's body, the ply slipping off the ledger and the bottom piece along with the body falling out the bottom of the coffin as it was lifted up.

A moment of collective panic ensued. Marg frowned. She is a worrier.

"I'm sure it will be fine," said Pat.

Marg's description of her liberal use of glue and screws eased my concern.

Marg says there have been great strides made lately in screw technology. Hex head screws that go in easily and you don't have to pre-drill.

"Oh My Goddess! Remember when we didn't have battery-operated drills?" I said. "I had to reach into my tool belt for a hammer and an awl to start the hole, and then screw in the screw with an old-fashioned slotted head screwdriver. In those days we used three-quarter-inch sheet metal screws to strap our electrical pipe to the wall. I had awesome forearms. People noticed my forearms."

"Yeah, I had an awesome back till I fell off that ladder," said Marg.

"And my knees were once awesome," said Pat, who was recovering slowly from a recent knee replacement.

We were just generally awesome.

Just the Facts, Forema'am

Why I Hate Firemen

Sitting in my favorite chair in the living room of my newly remodeled condo, I heard the violent breaking of glass. It sounded like someone was throwing bottles on the sidewalk with great force. I couldn't see anything out the front window so I put on shoes and went out there. That's when I saw flames shooting from the next-door neighbor's window, broken by the intense heat.

The year was 2009. After nearly a decade of work restoring and remodeling the three-unit building where I lived for 38 years in Bernal Heights, it nearly burned down that day.

I had brought my cell phone and immediately called 911. Someone had already called and the fire department said a truck was on the way. It seemed like it took forever but later I learned it had taken two minutes to come from our neighborhood firehouse at Holly Park.

A woman in a bathrobe emerged at a run from the ground level of the house next door. She had been in the shower when she smelled smoke. We knew that many people lived in the house. The owners of the single-family dwelling had divided it up into plywood cells with doors and locks, which they rented to Chinese immigrants, most of whom spoke no English. We had no idea how many people might be in the building.

I should add at this point that I hate firemen. Not firewomen, only the men. And not the firemen of color. Only the white men.

Whenever we have occasion to honor firefighters, which is lately often as the West has been burning up every year, I stand back and think to myself, I hate these mofos.

When I tell anyone I hate fire*men*, the reaction is always shock. "But there are some good men." And to this I say yes I know but they've gotta prove it to me, just as I had to constantly prove to my male coworkers over and over at work in construction that all women are not stupid and weak. In the meantime I'm sticking with my prejudice, formed by years of interaction with woman-hating racists in the San Francisco Fire Department. I may never get over it.

My hatred has roots in the decades-long fight to integrate women and people of color into the department, formed by listening to the stories of female firefighters who had to live in the firehouses where they were hated, denigrated, physically attacked and whose lives were in danger from the men they worked with.

The idea that firefighters are heroes to be worshipped not only had an unfortunate effect on the culture at the firehouses, inflating already overinflated egos. It also made opposing the white men more difficult. They used the positive stereotype to their advantage, calling on the testimony of citizens whose lives and property had been saved.

Before women fought their way into the SFFD, men of color experienced a racist culture and lack of safety in the department. The first Black firefighter entered the department in 1955 as the result of a lawsuit. The San Francisco firefighters' union, local 798, and its international affiliate, possibly the most racist union in the country, waged a campaign to keep minorities and women out of the department. Once they got in, the union and the white men did whatever they could to make their lives miserable. Swastikas, confederate flags, death threats, excrement in boots, tampering with safety equipment, and discriminatory entrance exams were some of the tactics. Robert Demmons, a Black firefighter, sued the department for discrimination and the lawsuit later included women and other men of color as plaintiffs.

Although agitation to include women in these well-paid jobs began in the 1970s, the first women did not enter the department until 1987. In the lawsuit, women were lucky to draw a judge who saw that breaking the gender barrier required strong measures. In 1986 US District Court Judge Marilyn Patel issued a consent decree requiring the department to hire ten percent women. The SFFD resisted the decree but they had to comply. The ten percent goal for women was met in 1997 and the decree lifted.

The person who files the lawsuit, whether in the trades or other professions, usually ends up dead or blacklisted, a martyr to the cause. Bob Demmons, who became president of the Black Firefighters Association (the BFA), went to work every day thinking he might be killed. Several attempts were made on his life. We affirmative action activists thought Bob would end up as our martyr, but instead he was appointed chief of the department in 1996 by Mayor Willie Brown. The department was still a mess and Bob worked closely with women and other men of color to change the culture. He knew he would have only a short time before the union and racists got him removed and he moved as quickly as he could to bring in and promote more women and minorities. I think Bob did more than any other individual to make firefighter jobs available to women. He's *my* hero.

We women did have a martyr, Anne Young, one of the first four women to be hired as firefighters, the first lesbian and also the first female lieutenant. Anne became the public face of women and so she endured the worst harassment.

I first met Anne at the Women's Training Center gym in San Francisco where we both worked out. An electrician, I was involved in the fight for affirmative action, agitating to get women into the construction trades and other male-dominated jobs. She was 18 and already clear about her life goal. She was training to be a firefighter. Anne took entry exams at fire departments all around California and she landed a job at the Daly City fire department where she did well. But Daly City is small, with very few fires and emergencies. She set her sights on the big city of San Francisco.

Anne was smart and strong and she already had experience working as a firefighter. She easily passed the entrance exam and became one of the first women to enter fire college. Harassment started immediately. The day that the first women graduated, before they even started working as firefighters, white men were picketing out in the street, saying that women had taken jobs from them.

Bob Demmons and Anne Young began to collaborate. They both wanted a department that reflects the percentages of population that it serves, that could speak all its languages, that would have women helping women. By that time most of the calls were medical emergencies, not fires.

At the time women first got in, San Francisco's 41 firehouses operated like a fraternity house row. Pornography was everywhere. Men watched porn on TV in the firehouses, which were scenes of hours-long cocktail parties and drinking contests. Bob showed Anne the granite wall with all the names of the firefighters killed in the line of duty. He pointed out names: "He was drunk, he was drunk, he was drunk." They were dead because they were drunk at a fire.

Female firefighters constantly had to choose. Did you go along with the culture and drink with the boys, or follow the rules which disallowed drinking, and risk isolation? One woman drank with the boys and passed out at dinner. She was terminated, and the female firefighters support group failed to offer any support. They didn't want to be associated with her.

Many women took the entrance tests and failed to pass. Many were terminated while on probation. One woman who made it in later committed suicide. The ones who stayed tried to be invisible, to not buck the culture. The other women in the SFFD did not necessarily support Anne.

As in construction, I don't fault women for how they choose to survive. We've developed many survival strategies. You have a choice of joining the culture or objecting. The women who tried to be invisible and didn't stick their necks out, who put up with the harassment or tried to be one of the guys, generally survived. Anne felt she couldn't go along to get along. She said she "felt pressure to make a choice every single day at work to represent every woman, represent every queer."

In the 1990s, before public shaming on the internet took hold, white male firefighters and retirees attacked females and minorities in a publication called the Smoke Eaters Gazette. They actually put in writing their horrible lies and distributed the paper to everyone in the department. We never learned who published it.

Anne was a union member, but when she found out the union was using her dues money to oppose affirmative action, she resigned from local 798 and joined the BFA, a slap in the face to the union and the white men.

A watershed moment came in 1988 when the women in the SFFD and the BFA drove a fire truck in the gay parade, a first for the department, known for its homophobic culture. Anne Young was driving the truck. Cheers went up from the crowd. The Black firefighters stood with the gay community politically in that moment.

It took some courage for the straight Black men to march in the parade. I was watching from the street and I cried. People on the sidelines were yelling, "Hey-hey, ho-ho, racism has got to go." The guys were crying. Everyone was crying. It was an historic event.

Anne did well on tests. She had taken and passed many. When the test for lieutenant came up she was urged to take it by the lawyers and the BFA. The chief of the department called her into his office and told her she could have anything she wanted if she *didn't* take the test.

In retrospect, she said, taking the lieutenants' test and promoting was a mistake, the beginning of the end of her career. As a new lieutenant she worked a different firehouse every day. Some days the entire crew would call in sick, sending a clear message they didn't want to work for her. Death threats were common. But when men on her crew tried to throw her off a roof, that was her breaking point. They could have gotten away with her murder. Firefighters fall off roofs. No one would have known she was pushed.

After that, Anne kept going to work, but she felt she could no longer do her job competently.

I've seen this happen to other women in male-dominated jobs when the everyday level of stress becomes too much for the body to bear. Your mind tells you to go to work but at some point your body rebels. You get sick or injured and you can no longer go to work. After she was nearly killed, Anne had what she called a nervous breakdown. One day she just couldn't get out of bed. I think this was her body protecting her from harm.

Anne filed a lawsuit and there was a trial where she was called upon to paint the SFFD with a broad brush of discriminatory treatment. She didn't get to talk about how much she loved the job, working with a team, saving lives. It had been her dream and she was really good at her job. She wasn't able to focus on the good men who helped her. But, on the whole, even the good guys had refused to stand up for her and risk retaliation from the bad actors. They enabled the harassers.

Three years after filing suit, in 1995, Anne won the lawsuit and was awarded $300,000. But her career as a firefighter was finished. She lost her income, she lost her house. Trauma had infected her like a disease.

I thought of this history as I stood on the sidewalk and watched the house next door to mine burn. When the first fire truck arrived at the scene, the first firefighter who jumped off was a woman I rec-ognized, Nicol Juratavac. She was working as a lieutenant that day. Among the firefighters were several women and men of color. One, a Chinese man, was the only person able to communicate with the next-door building's residents. Then a car pulled up with another woman I recognized, Denise Newman. She was working that day as a battalion chief. Of course, by that time in 2009 the chief of the de-partment was a female, Joanne Hayes-White, appointed by Mayor Newsom in 2004.

Along with a congregation of feminist activists, I had shown up at city hall the day her appointment was announced. Newsom ap-pointed a female police chief as well, which gave us all high hopes that the asshole culture could be turned around. And I do think some progress was made. Hayes-White stayed on the job for 15 years, long after Newsom had moved on up the political ladder. The SFFD wom-en often clashed with her, but in general her policies and promotions were female friendly. Heather Fong, the police chief, hung in for ten years before the white men and the police union were finally able to run her out.

Wringing my hands and worrying that my newly remodeled building was about to go up in flames, I was grateful for the SFFD. And I had an epiphany: decades of fighting to make the department reflect San Francisco's diverse population had paid off. The fire department had been integrated.

Now, a decade later, many of those first women have retired from the department with generous pensions. Some of them struggle with PTSD from years of harassment. Yes, the culture in the firehouses has changed for the better, but discrimination and harassment are still present. Anti-affirmative action laws passed in the 1990s make targeted recruitment illegal and make it difficult for California public safety entities to maintain the minimum number of women and minority employees that had been required by SFFD's consent decree. There's no guarantee that the department will not revert back to its old white male culture.

However, the new chief of the department, appointed in 2019, Jeanine Nicholson, a lesbian cancer survivor and also burn survivor, gives me hope that the department has changed for good. Still, I haven't forgiven those white men.

I thank Bob Demmons, and especially Anne Young who sacrificed her career so other women could become firefighters. They were truly change makers.

Fighting for Gender Neutral Language

As a young reader I took umbrage at authors who insisted on referring to mankind and men when discussing all humans including women. It didn't help when librarians and teachers patiently explained to me that the words mankind and men were meant to include women. I didn't believe it and I just stopped reading those writers. But I was still angry at the mainstream ideology. You couldn't escape it.

When I found feminism, I found sisters who agreed with me. Women were being left out of history and the present by the use of sexist language. Several feminists developed genderless languages and pronoun replacements, which unfortunately never caught on. Today transgender activists seem to agree on replacing *she* and *he* with *they*.

Gender specific job titles have always rankled women who work in or aspire to work in male-dominated jobs. If a job title ends in man like lineman, mailman, policeman, or draughtsman, we get the point that women do not belong and are not welcome in these jobs. Girls and young women understand that they should seek careers elsewhere.

Sisters in the Brotherhood

I was just lucky that electrician, my own trade, is already gender neutral. Visiting Mexico, I was delighted to learn that *electrician* in Spanish is *electricista*. We haven't had to fight battles about *carpenter, plumber, ironworker* or *sheet metal worker*.

But each of these trades trains its workers in an apprenticeship program. When the apprentice graduates from the program they "turn out" as a *journeyman*, meaning they are free to travel for work outside their union local. Tradeswomen have replaced that term with *journeyworker* or *journeywoman*. We laughingly invented the term *forema'am* to replace *foreman*, but there's no reason we can't use any number of gender neutral terms like crew boss or crew leader.

Then there's the brotherhood issue. Most construction unions are brotherhoods by title and most have refused to consider changing to a gender neutral term. Instead of International Brotherhood of Electrical Workers, how about International Union of Electrical Workers? Over the years sister electricians have floated the idea of getting the international to change its title to a more inclusive one, but the men in power refuse to entertain the idea. In artful protest I wrote my dues checks to the "International Sisterhood of Electrical Workers." No one ever said anything and the checks were always cashed. I guess the bank doesn't care what term we use.

The one union to do battle with its membership about the term brotherhood was the Teamsters, 30 percent of whose 1.4 million members are women. A proposal to change brotherhood to a more inclusive term was put forward by the progressive president Ron Carey at an international meeting in 1996. Members were consulted about the idea and debated the issue for months in union publications, but Carey's rival, James P. Hoffa opposed the change. He famously said, "It's gender neutral. The definition of brotherhood is that it's neutral." Supporters of inclusion lost the vote, Hoffa took over as president, and the Teamsters remain a brotherhood.

Taking an Axe to Fireman

Feminists have spent many years trying to retrain reporters and speakers to use the term firefighter instead of fireman. Mostly we have been successful, but it takes letters to writers in all genres to make a change. The New Yorker magazine has been one recalcitrant actor. I think those New Yorkers must look at their own backward fire department and think, "Why should I use a gender neutral term? There *are* no women." And this is almost true. But their response *should* be embarrassment at their city's failure to integrate its fire department.

I've written many letters to my daily newspaper, the San Francisco Chronicle, about this issue over the years. One of the most grievous examples was a column by Rob Morse, a writer with liberal politics whom I read regularly while he was published. After a big fire destroyed one of the buildings at the old Ghirardelli chocolate factory, Morse thanked the brave "firemen" who extinguished the blaze. Ironically, the photo of one of the working firefighters that appeared on the front page of the Chronicle was a picture of a female. You just couldn't tell her gender because of all the protective gear she wore. My outraged letter to the editor was published but only with poor edits which made me look stupid. Still, it brought the issue to the editors' attention. The Chronicle eventually changed its style to firefighter.

One example of the prevalence of this misuse of the word is in the comics. I'm a regular reader of the comic Luann, whose central character is a teenage girl (kudos!). I was heartened when the artist, Greg Evans, introduced a female character who becomes a firefighter and eventually dates Luann's older brother. In the comic she also must contend with an abusive boyfriend, an issue that doesn't often make it into the comics. Still, the artist continued to use the term *fireman* even when referring to that character. In my letter I praised the artist for creating this female character and tried to explain how using a gender neutral descriptor would make her an even better role model for girls who read the comic. Presumably mine was not the only complaint. The comic eventually changed the term.

The firefighter argument is closest to my heart. Feminist activists in San Francisco battled for 16 years with the SFFD before women were allowed to work as firefighters. Then for 12 years I was partnered with a female firefighter who eventually became the SF fire marshal. I don't always fault women in the gunsights for not fighting this battle. Women working in a male-dominated culture have to pick our battles and descriptive terms may not be the most important issue. That's why it is imperative that feminist activists outside these workplaces pile on to push for change. When I worked in the SF Department of Building Inspection I had a cordial relationship with the fire inspectors I worked with (that's where I met my now ex-partner.) I didn't hesitate to correct their language. When they didn't change, I would greet them in the elevator, "How are the firewomen today?" That got their attention.

During my stint as the "fire marshal's wife," I saw these guys at parties and social events. Just like in the building trades, they had no second thoughts about insulting me or women in general, right to my face. When you first hear: "Women can't do the job, women shouldn't be in the fire department," etc., you are shocked, but the fortunate thing about continually being subjected to insults (as with sexual harassment) is that it gives you practice in responding. I was never great at quick retorts, but I got better with lots of practice.

My ex-partner said: "Every time I read the word *fireman*, it's like a punch in the stomach. It reminds me of when my brother (four years older, bigger, and stronger) would punch me, then hold me at arm's length by putting his palm on my forehead and I'd be swinging away at him, never able to land a punch back."

Fishing for Fishers

Lately I've been addressing writers about the term *fisherman*. *Fisher* is such an obvious and easy choice and I can't understand why speakers and writers are so resistant to change. It's not just men. Women are sometimes just as argumentative. Except there's not a very good argument. "We've always done it that way," the typical response, just doesn't cut it.

The last few times I've written to the Chronicle's writers about the term *fisherman* (I love that the writer's email address is listed at the end of the article), one didn't reply, one wrote back to say simply "thank you," and one wrote that she had thought of *fisherman* as a gender neutral term.

Perhaps the reason this choice of words is ignored is that the fishing industry has been floundering and dying now for decades. Few choose to be fishers anymore, but I personally know women who integrated this industry in the 1970s and women who continue to make a living fishing. It's still an important industry on the California coast, so the Chronicle runs fishing stories often. In recent stories, writers have used both the terms *fisher* and *fisherman*. I think my letters must have made an impact. They seem to be breaking their readers in slowly.

One wonders what journalists would think if all reporters were referred to as "newsmen." Oh, wait. They were. And not that long ago.

News flash: From a story in *The Guardian* about the discovery of four new elements in the periodic table: "This article was amended. The reference to the new elements being "manmade" was changed to "synthetic" to follow Guardian style guidance on the use of gender neutral terms."

What I Know About Stereotyping

The culture of the construction site was shaped by men. No women had been involved in its creation and so we had to negotiate the best we could. I said to myself I had a father and three brothers; I should be able to fit in. I'd been a tomboy as a kid and thought I knew how to hang with males of the species. Every new job, each with a new group of guys, held new challenges.

I quickly learned that my coworkers thought women were incapable of doing the physically challenging work of construction. They brought to work a stereotype of women as stupid, whiny, useless, money-grubbing weaklings who needed a man to give them worth in the world. (Most of these guys were divorced and still angry at ex-wives.) They repeated to me an old saying: If this work was easy, women and children could do it. Something told me that when they repeated it to each other, the word they used was not women.

"Cunt," whispered the ironworker tying rebar next to me as I tied electrical pipe to it. Then he quickly moved on. After I got over the shock, here's what I thought: "Ironworkers are a bunch of cowardly sexist dickheads."

My coworkers told me women weren't good partners on the job because we couldn't be trusted to hold up our end of a 300-pound piece of floor duct. We were all afraid of heights, we didn't know how to swing a hammer and hit anything. We were just there to get a man. Our presence on the job would cost the contractor money since it took us twice as long to complete a task. When criticized we would cry, so they had to be careful what they said to us. (Too bad that didn't translate to not insulting us.) Their worth was predicated on our worthlessness, our lack of merit. You are only as tall as the person you are stepping on.

I went to work each day with the objective of overturning the old stereotype. I was usually the only female on the job, and very conscious that I could embody a new improved stereotype. I worked hard but was careful not to work so hard that I'd be accused of breaking down conditions and brown-nosing the employer. I tried to work just as fast as they did, but not faster. I picked up my end of the floor duct and used lifting skills to save my back, while thinking to myself that nobody should have to lift 300 pounds of anything. I was not afraid of heights, but if I had been, I would not have admitted it. I never cried, even when I felt like it.

A worker was welcomed into the construction culture in a backhanded manner. You didn't know whether you were being dissed or included. Race and ethnicity as well as gender were called out with jokes and put-downs. How one responded was noted. You were supposed to go along to get along.

The men could be empathetic while at the same time expressing homophobia, sexism and racism. I tried to come out as a lesbian whenever the opportunity arose because I was convinced this honesty made the job easier for me. On one job I worked with a traveler* from Arizona. We were assigned to tape connectors and boxes in the trailer while we waited for the deck to be readied for the electrical crew, so we had time to chat. He told me he and his wife were in town for a few months. She worked as a nurse in a hospital in Oakland and the place was overrun with faggots. She was disgusted, he said. Here was my opportunity! I admitted to being a dyke and noted that fags were a lot more fun to work with than his sorry ass. At that he did an about-face. He needed to make a confession too. He acknowledged that he was an alcoholic, that he was in recovery and that he was letting me in on the secret. That made us even, and we were friends from then on.

Ethnic slurs were thrown at people with what almost seemed like a try at love. Wetback, Chink, Dago were used inclusively, like welcome to our club, this is your identity. If I didn't object in the beginning, my nickname would be Girl. I objected, but not to every slight. You had to pick your battles. I let them know I wasn't keen on sexist or racist remarks. No one ever said the N word in racially-mixed company, maybe because they didn't want to risk getting the shit beat out of them. The exception was travelers who came from sister union locals in the South, but they only used the word when conversing with whites. Talking about football, one remarked, "I never understood why anyone would want to watch a bunch of n*****s running around a field." The Northern white guys on the crew were silent after that. Maybe they were seriously considering that football was no longer a white game. Or maybe they were silent on my account and would have agreed with the cracker if I hadn't been there. I hope it was because they were so appalled they were speechless.

The Southern travelers were a different breed—bigots who bragged about killing cops and evading taxes. All white. The story was told about one guy that he kept a length of 000 wire under the seat of his truck and had once used it on a cop's head. One day he drug up** and asked for his check. He was on the run, they said. White trash and dangerous.

As soon as you walked onto the job you were typecast and few of us minorities were exempt. On one job I had a Jewish crew leader. I knew he was Jewish when others on the job started making gas chamber and oven jokes. Jewish men—at least out Jewish men—were rare on the construction site, although I knew many Jewish women who worked in construction. This guy had been a carpenter and later got into the electrician apprenticeship. He was a skilled mechanic and a competent crew boss with an upbeat attitude. He let the jokes slide off.

The job was an interior remodel of the Hyatt Regency hotel in San Francisco's Embarcadero Center. Cozy and insulated, we worked on an upper floor of the high-rise, piping in the ceiling, running up and down ladders. The construction crew would assemble in the basement in the mornings and ride the service elevator up to our floor together. The hotel pastry chef, a stern Austrian, came to work at the same time and rode the elevator with us. He never spoke to us, we figured because he thought himself better than a bunch of construction workers. An unflattering stereotype of Austrians immediately took root in my mind. Austrians equal Nazis. Our crew began to refer to him as Herr Pastry. My crew boss always spoke to him. Good morning or how are you this morning. The pastry chef may have nodded but he never spoke or smiled. It became a game. The Jew would force the Nazi to acknowledge us lower class plebes (the irony was that we union workers probably made way more money than he did.)

Our IBEW contract gave us a half-hour lunch break 12 to 12:30 and one ten-minute coffee break, which we took at 10am. I usually brought a bagel with cream cheese for break. I'd be starving by 10 even after eating a huge breakfast at 6:30. On jobs where the ten minutes was taken literally, I found I barely had time to down the bagel, which required some chewing, and to wash it down with my thermos of tea. This job was a bit looser. Coffee break might last 15 minutes.

"It's too short," I whined to no one in particular while standing on a ladder with my head in the ceiling. The piece of EMT*** I'd just cut didn't fit and I'd have to cut it again.

"What a thing to tell a man!" came back to me from the Irish carpenter crew boss whose head was the only one I could see up there. That made me smile. Irish guys—full of blarney.

"Break time," someone yelled, and I looked down to see coffee being served in a fancy silver service with a huge plate of pastries beside it. The gift had come from the pastry chef, and for the rest of that job we had complimentary coffee and pastries at 10am, thanks to the persistent civility of our boss. My stereotype of Austrians crumbled. I'm still waiting for help with my prejudice against iron-workers and white Southern men.

*Travelers follow the work around the country when work at home is slow.

**To drag up is to quit the job.

***Electrical Metallic Tubing, a kind of pipe used in the electrical industry.

Men Making Men Look Bad

When I worked construction, often as the only female on the job-site, I was very aware that I represented all women, and any mistake I made would make my whole gender look bad in the eyes of my male coworkers. Unsurprisingly, the men had no such concern about making their own gender look bad. Apparently they didn't care what we thought of them, but we were just as quick to form stereotypes as they were. This essay appeared in Tradeswomen Magazine *in 1983 and I'd bet it still applies today.*

Ask any tradeswoman to name the most difficult part of her job and the answer most likely will not be hard work, cold weather or dirt. Unless she works in a woman-owned company, she'll probably say, "the men."

When we walk onto a construction site or into an all-male shop, we enter enemy territory, and while it may not always be a war zone, we must be prepared for the defense. Chances are the lone woman will be subjected to harassment. The men can be condescending, racist, hateful, misogynous, resentful, obscene, dangerous, verbally abusive, and physically intimidating. They can also be helpful, fatherly, overprotective, and sometimes democratic, and genuinely friendly.

Here are some hints to help distinguish one type from another and some suggestions for preparing your defense.

The Know-It-All

He gets his ego gratification from explaining to others how to do things. You will be his favorite target, since he assumes women know nothing and must be told everything, and also that we will be too polite to tell him to shove off.

It is important to recognize this type in the beginning and assert yourself. Your coworker is suspect when he gives blatantly wrong advice, such as instructing you to insert a hacksaw blade with the teeth facing toward the handle. He may also give himself away by fabricating details about a job you're familiar with.

Once discovered, he should never be believed. You'll inevitably be sorry for taking his bad advice. Try to ignore him when he's talking, nod thoughtfully and go on with your task. As an attention-getting device, he may try to take tools out of your hands. In that case, never relinquish your tools. Patiently admonish him to find his own project and leave you alone. When all else fails, grab the tools forcefully and yell, "Get your hands off my tools."

Momma's Boy

The first day on the job he'll seek you out and confess: 1) His wife doesn't understand him, their sex life is terribly unsatisfying, and would you like to have a drink after work; 2) His wife is divorcing him; he's hurt, dismayed, and convinced he's done nothing to deserve this treatment; 3) She got the kids in the divorce, and now she wants child support, which he's sure she'll throw away on expensive clothes instead of feeding the kids; 4) He beats his wife but she deserves it and he wants your approval.

Resist the impulse to mother this man. Hold back when tempted to cook him dinner, or even to pat him on the back. Don't offer your shoulder when he looks like he might cry; treat him like any other coworker. Let him know there's no excuse to avoid child support payments, or for mistreating his wife. Don't compromise your views or offer a sympathetic ear in exchange for his "opening up" and confessing feelings. You will probably discover you don't really want to know that much about his personal life.

The Fatherly Type

If this older coworker treats you like his daughter, his "fatherly" advice might be worth the indignity of your role. If he's a skilled tradesman and seems willing to pass along tricks of the trade, do take advantage and listen. If you feel obliged to refrain from swearing and spitting around this old-fashioned gentleman, remember you'll be spared dirty jokes and misogynistic banter. But don't hesitate to explain that your own father recognizes you're an adult woman and doesn't address you as "girl" or "young lady."

The Yahoo

Give this gorilla a hundred pounds to carry and he'll ask for more. Whenever there's a question about whether to use brains or brawn to accomplish a task, he'll try to prove there's as much muscle in his head as in his arms.

The Yahoo hasn't yet developed a sense of his own mortality and is almost always very young (the older guys have already hurt their backs if they've survived at all.) Besides making coworkers (and especially female ones) look bad by competing with them instead of maintaining a reasonable work pace, he's downright dangerous. He'll be the one calling safety-minded workers sissies while hanging off a building three stories up without a safety belt. Don't get seduced into playing his macho game. Stay clear of him if at all possible. In any case, you will most likely see his work later when you're called in to go back and repair his multitude of mistakes.

The Short Crew Boss

This guy is Caesar, Hitler or Napoleon in a hard hat. The short man's pigheaded, pugnacious, and generally mean reputation acquires a new dimension on the construction site. He probably entered the trade to prove he could be just as macho as the big boys, so seeing a woman master his trade is devastating. When this guy has made it to crew boss, you may have to practice turning a deaf ear to his squeals. In the meantime, if you're bigger than he is, get your kicks from besting him at tasks requiring brute force or just standing next to him and looking down.

The Liberal

He thinks that declaring his support for the ERA exempts him from any criticism. Once publicly allied with the progressive element, he can be expected to barrage you with any number of racist, sexist and homophobic remarks. A few elementary feminist platitudes are deemed fair exchange for offensive "in" jokes. He'll tell you he never means to insult, then wonder aloud why feminists don't have a sense of humor.

This character's contradictions make him more insidious than the average sexist. Because he often knows the right words to mouth, his subtle put-downs leave you wondering whose side he's on. For example, unlike the admitted misogynist who'll tell you women don't belong in the trades, the liberal will make the right assumptions with qualifications: "All in all, women do pretty well, but I've never worked with one who could (supply your own skill) as well as a man."

The liberal wants your approval and sometimes your friendship because it reinforces his own open-minded, progressive image of himself. This can work to your advantage as long as you maintain a proper amount of mistrust. He can turn out to be an ally or an enemy, but you can't count on either. In any case, while dealing with the liberal is endlessly frustrating, you may be successful in changing his outward behavior, which could be a real bonus on the job.

How to Avoid Reproduction

I had a hysterectomy in 1975 when I was 25 years old. I didn't have cancer or uterine cysts. What I had was dysmenorrhea, or menstrual cramps.

This was an operation I had actively pursued and I felt lucky to get it, taking advantage of the remnants of the US Public Health system before it was abolished by the Reagan administration.

Buckets of Blood

Like 80 percent of women, I suffered from menstrual pain. Like 10 percent of women, the pain was severe enough to disrupt my life. Menstruation, since the age of 13, had been a trial for me that only worsened by the time I got to high school. Huge gobs of clotted blood would gush from my body every three weeks for a week at a time. The pain was debilitating. By the time I got to college I was unable to work for two days a month when my period was at its worst, a terrible embarrassment for a young militant feminist who passionately believed that women are men's equal.

In high school I had friends who got pregnant and had to drop out of school, young women who gave up babies for adoption or had to get married. The lesson was clear to me: don't get pregnant or you won't get an education. Pregnancy, and marriage too, seemed like a kind of death. I was determined not to ruin my life. In high school I never had sex, but there wasn't any boy I wanted to have sex with.

I asked my parents what they would do if I got pregnant. My mother said they would help me get an abortion. Much later, after she died, I learned that my mother had had at least two abortions. She never told me, even during the feminist campaign led by Ms. Magazine in which famous women publicly admitted to their abortions.

How I Got The Pill

By the time I got to college, I was embarrassed to be a virgin, so I set out to remedy that state of affairs. I was hanging out with a boy I met in the bacteriology lab who seemed interested in me. I asked him if he wanted to have sex and he was happy to oblige. We shook on the deal. First, though, I wanted to be sure I was protected from getting pregnant and I didn't want to leave that up to him. The Pill was newly available and I convinced a doctor at the student health clinic to give me a prescription. The year was 1968.

The Pill wasn't all it was cracked up to be. The Pill makes your body think it's pregnant, which meant for me morning sickness, bloating and sore breasts. And the periods were still bad. Only many years later did I learn that it's not necessary to have a period when you're on the Pill. That was the Catholic Church's doing, part of a deal between the church and pill makers. The church agreed not to oppose the marketing of the Pill for birth control if certain requirements were met, one being that periods stayed. Even though I was never a Catholic, the church had an unseen hand in my reproductive life. I was pissed when I learned that I could have controlled my painful periods by taking the Pill throughout the month if not for the Catholic Church. But at least by the late 60s the Pill was available to me and other unmarried women (for a time it was only prescribed to married women—another church requirement.)

I'm Going to Throw Up

My menstrual periods continued to worsen, causing vomiting

and diarrhea as well as pain. I developed a long-term relationship with the student health center, but they began to tell me and other female students that painful periods were not a health issue and that we would not be treated there. If I told them the reason, they would refuse to take me in, so I worked out a strategy where I would run into the clinic and say to the receptionist, "I'm going to throw up." That got me into a room with a pan, and I was able to see a doctor. Not that they could do much for me. They gave me painkillers, usually a shot of something, and sent me home, where I would lie in bed for the rest of the day, still in pain, just duller pain. I was still useless.

This was no way to live. I resolved to do something about this devitalizing state of affairs. I began reading everything I could get on the subject of menstruation and birth control, frequenting the medical library at Washington State University. I learned about the effects of the female hormones estrogen and progesterone and how they control the menstrual cycle. I only understood about half of the medical terms, but could make out the general ideas. It seemed from my reading that I might have something called endometriosis, where the lining of the uterus gets into the body cavity and responds to hormones by bleeding into your insides.

At that time in the 1960s, research was still going on to refine the Pill. I read about different types of pills I could try and I convinced the one female doctor in the student health center to let me experiment on myself. She prescribed a kind of progesterone pill, but, as with previous experiments, the side effects cancelled out the positive. One day when I lay with my feet up suffering intense cramping and pain, I popped a progesterone pill. The pain stopped within minutes! Progesterone, my savior! Why didn't women know about this? Why don't women still know about this?

Did the medical establishment want women to suffer just as the Catholic Church did? Reading the book, *The Pill*, I later discovered that developers of the Pill claimed to be developing a treatment for dysmenorrhea because it sounded better than birth control to the church and the powers that be. Too bad they didn't tell the women like me who actually suffered from dysmenorrhea.

Taking Control of Our Bodies

My relationship with the medical establishment at WSU was not only based on my own complaints. Along with my Women's Liberation group I had been working to help women get reproductive care. We set up a counseling center in the student union and I became a volunteer counselor. The typical "client" was a student who'd had sex once and gotten pregnant. She might be a rape victim. She'd had little or no sex education in school; she had never talked to anyone about sex or reproduction. She was confused and embarrassed. One young woman was so mortified that she ran out of the room soon after she'd walked in.

We set up underground networks to help women procure abortions and we worked with doctors in the community to provide reproductive care in the town and at the university. A book written by activists in Boston, *Our Bodies Ourselves*, reflected feminist organizing all over the country. We were inspired to learn about our bodies and take control of our own health care.

During this time, women in Washington State organized to overturn the law criminalizing abortion and my Women's Liberation group worked on that ballot campaign. Abortion became legal in Washington in 1970, three years before the Roe v. Wade Supreme Court decision legalized abortion nationwide. Washington was the first state in the country to make abortion legal by referendum.

If Men Could Get Pregnant,

Abortion Would Be a Sacrament

My search for the perfect method of birth control continued. I never liked condoms and felt that getting men to use them was not worth the effort, although I always carried one in my wallet. Still, I thought that men should be required to take responsibility for birth control. A popular feminist poster showed a picture of a big-bellied man and the slogan: "If men could get pregnant, abortion would be a sacrament." Feminists wanted control of our own reproductive lives. We wanted the freedom to have sex without guilt and without consequences, just like men had. But we certainly didn't want to depend on abortion as a primary method of birth control. We wanted contraception that didn't hurt and wasn't a big hassle.

I Got IUD'd

IUDs (intrauterine devices) were becoming a popular form of birth control. It seemed like a great alternative to the Pill. You had to have it inserted by a doctor, but then presumably you never had to think about it again. Not so with me.

There were many types of IUDs, but the most popular at that time was the Dalkon Shield. I went to a health clinic in the community to have it inserted. The doctor there was an older man whom I'd worked with to help provide women with reproductive care. He was inserting the Dalkon Shield into many women's uteruses. That part went smoothly, but soon I was in pain, which continued to worsen. The pain was constant. The pain radiated from the core of my body out to my limbs. No part of my body was free of the pain. I thought to myself at the time that I could not imagine any pain worse than that cramping, and I have never experienced anything close to it in my life. My uterus was trying to expel the IUD and so I was in constant labor. (Needless to say, sex was the last thing on my mind.) But the Dalkon Shield was made to resist. You had to have it removed by a doctor, and after a couple of weeks of agony I did. When I visited the mild-mannered old doctor again, he told me of anecdotal evidence that women were having some problems with the Dalkon Shield. He emphasized anecdotal. He was a science-based guy after all, and there were no studies. Still, I could see the worried look on his face and I celebrated being IUD free.

Later, of course, we learned of the terrible problems caused by the Dalkon Shield. Women suffered from pelvic inflammatory disease. Women were made infertile. Women died. We had been experimental subjects. I joined a class action lawsuit against the manufacturer and eventually received $750, a big sum of money for me then. The manufacturer, A.H. Robins Co., went bankrupt.

Birth control never failed me; I never got pregnant. But I was pissed that it was so difficult. Later, when I sat down to chronicle my torturous, painful attempts to keep from getting pregnant I got angry all over again. Even for a relatively privileged white, college-educated woman, birth control had been arduous.

The People's Health Care System

In 1973 I left the little college burg of Pullman for the big city of Seattle. But I had carefully laid the foundation for continuing reproductive care in my new home.

The People's Health Care System, a grassroots response to inadequate health care, acted like a safety net, doctoring the poor and insurance-free. Led by the Black Panther Party, activists in Seattle had created the system, which later included the Women's Clinic at the YWCA where I volunteered, and community-built clinics in the city's poorer underserved neighborhoods. Country Doctor, one of the first community clinics, is still operating.

Seattle still maintained a merchant seamen's hospital, part of the US Public Health Service, where medical care was free. Over the years, military dependents, Coast Guard personnel, Native Americans and medically indigent citizens were added to the patient load. The PHS hospital in Seattle by the 1970s was a center of people's health care activism.

I arrived in Seattle at an auspicious time for public health care. I had documented well my battle with endometriosis (or whatever it was—I never got a diagnosis except the general term dysmenorrhea.) My doctor at the WSU health center had given a written recommendation for a hysterectomy. And I made connections with the network of activist health care providers by volunteering at the Women's Clinic. They put me in touch with a doctor who agreed to oversee the operation.

The US Public Health Service

The Seattle public health hospital building, an imposing Art Deco edifice built in 1931, still crowns Beacon Hill in the south part of the city. I was admitted to a ward reserved for women undergoing reproductive surgery. The huge open room housed perhaps 15 or 20 beds. You could pull a curtain to separate yourself from the others, but I wanted to be part of the action. I made an effort to meet and talk to the other patients, and the atmosphere was friendly. Most of the women were wives of Navy men in for hysterectomies or removal of ovarian cysts. But one young woman told me she was a fisher and was in for a (free) abortion.

This was a teaching hospital. Young interns performed many of the surgeries and probably also did mine. I engaged one of the female interns, asking about endometriosis and hormone studies. Her answer chilled me. Few studies existed regarding the female reproductive system, she said. "We just don't know very much." At that time women were seldom the subjects of medical studies, which were almost all about men.

As I was being wheeled into surgery and before the drugs took effect, I thought to myself that I should have told my parents about the hysterectomy. I had been advised that there was a small chance I wouldn't wake up from the general anesthesia. What if I were to die? My poor mother! I was her only daughter, a very selfish daughter. But I'd been afraid my mother would try to dissuade me and I hadn't wanted to have the argument with her. I felt strongly that this was my personal decision.

At that time there was unbelievable pressure on women to have children. Everyone told you you'd change your mind when the maternal instinct kicked in. "Every woman wants children!" "It's in your genes." "You are a freak if you don't want children," we were told repeatedly. Young women were not allowed to have hysterectomies because doctors thought we didn't know our own minds. At the public health hospital they believed me when I told them I really didn't want children. I never changed my mind.

Only my uterus was coming out, not ovaries. The interns had explained to me that they would try to do a vaginal hysterectomy. They wouldn't cut my abdominal muscles unless they had to. So I wouldn't know the result until I came out of surgery and the anesthesia wore off. Some of the women in the ward had pretty ugly incisions and of course I had to see them all. As it turned out, the hysterectomy was vaginal, so I was left with no scar.

Because I got an infection (a common thing for younger people, they said), I had to live in the ward for 12 days. In that time I got to know the staff and the patients pretty well. I wanted to know how they funded the surgeries of people like me who were not seamen, fishers or Navy. They told me money came from a fund for special or interesting cases. I thought that was odd since my case seemed pretty routine. Later I learned that hospital Director Dr. Willard P. Johnson had found an obscure regulation in the Public Health Service Act that allowed a director to allocate up to five percent of the care offered at the facility for "special studies." The provision was intended to allow the admission of patients with rare diseases for the benefit of the medical education program. Dr. Johnson decided to interpret it differently, admitting every person referred from a community clinic as a special studies patient. This decision was the origin of the long-standing affiliation with the region's community health centers.

The PHS hospital, because of its close relationship with the neighborhood clinics, became the center of the People's Health Care System in Seattle. It was part of a vital community movement for control of our own health care, which had far reaching effects. Through our activism women did gain a measure of control and also won changes in the health care system. The women's clinics in Seattle, set up to help women access abortion and reproductive care, continued to operate for many years. But our most important community partner, the PHS hospital and its federally funded public health care system, died a tortured death.

Republicans Shut It Down

The Republican assault on health care is not a new phenomenon. When politicians grouse that we can't afford Medicare for all, they forget that the US once actually had a well-run public health care system. It was destroyed by Ronald Reagan.

The Seattle PHS hospital was part of a network of public health hospitals and federally-funded free clinics all over the country. Soon after he took office Reagan shut down all the public hospitals. In Seattle he had to fight the community as well as Washington's powerful Senators Warren Magnuson and Henry Jackson, and Seattle's mayor, but Reagan pretty quickly won the fight.

The assault was unremitting. Between 1980 and 1991, more than 250 community health centers were closed, 309 rural hospitals and 294 urban hospitals were shuttered. Nearly one million Native Americans lost access to Indian Health Service care when eligibility was narrowed. Reagan's budget cuts hacked at school lunches, Medicaid, the food stamp program, WIC and AFDC. He caused a two percent increase in the poverty rate, and the number of children in poverty rose nearly three percent.

Forty years later it's clear that the Republicans' answer to the prospect of socialized medicine is, for a growing number of Americans, no health care at all. And the attacks on women's reproductive care continue with the recent Supreme Court decision allowing religious exemptions for birth control. Soon Roe v. Wade may be overturned and we'll be back where we started. For a brief window in time American women enjoyed the right to control our bodies and reproduction. Now it looks as if that window may be closing.

Making America White Again
Contemplating the Roots of Racism in My Hometown

Americans should not be surprised by the rise of nativism prompted by the rhetoric of the far right. White supremacy, xenophobia and red baiting have a long history in the United States. My hometown makes a good example.

It was said that my grandfather, Ben Wick, and William O. Douglas were the only two Democrats in Yakima, Washington in the early 1920s. Or perhaps they were the only two *admitted* Democrats. In my hometown at that time being a Democrat automatically labeled you as a Communist.

William O., then known as Orville Douglas, grew up in Yakima but as a young man left to find his fortune in the East. FDR appointed him to head the new Securities and Exchange Commission and then to the Supreme Court. He became the longest serving U.S. Supreme Court Justice and Yakima's most famous native son, but the town reviled him. The New Deal Democrat was far too liberal for Yakima.

My grandfather, a Norwegian immigrant, traveled with his family—my Swedish grandmother and their four daughters—to Yakima in 1921. He and Orville Douglas met at Yakima High School where they both were teachers.

When my mother was growing up in the 1920s and 30s, Yakima, with a population of about 20,000, was a conservative place. Today, with about 91,000 people, it remains a red blot in a blue state. Washington's population is concentrated on the West Coast around Seattle. Rural eastern Washington is another world. In the 2016 and the 2020 presidential elections Yakima County went for

Trump/Pence.

Yakima's story is not unfamiliar. It's been reenacted in countless towns across this continent. Catholic missionaries had settled in the Valley and white settlers followed in the 1850s as the US Army drove the indigenous population onto a nearby reservation. The Native Americans had fiercely resisted in what were known as the Indian Wars. The Yakama (the tribe changed to this spelling) Indian reservation is home to several different indigenous groups that were forced to settle there in what we call the Lower Valley, a few miles south of the town of Yakima. The sagebrush country with fertile volcanic soil was partly developed and irrigated by Japanese immigrant farmers who began arriving before the turn of the 20th century.

Researching what life was like in my hometown in this period, I found a book written by Thomas Heuterman, who was my journalism professor at Washington State University. *The Burning Horse: The Japanese Experience in the Yakima Valley 1920-1942* documents discrimination against the Japanese community in Wapato, a town on the Yakama reservation where the farmers leased land from the tribe. In emails Prof. Heuterman told me he had been surprised to find what his research showed: a long history of racism and exclusion in the Yakima Valley. Japanese farmers in the Valley were persecuted relentlessly. Their houses, barns and crops were bombed and burned.

Heuterman grew up in Wapato. He wrote: "I went into the project predicting that the Valley Japanese were an exception among all the prejudice of the era. That's what I remembered as a child from my folks' attitudes. But, as you know, I found just the opposite. Most of the Nisei (second generation) who have read the book also didn't know that racism was going on; their folks had protected them from that too."

Newspapers stoked the fires of racism. Prof. Heuterman's research focused on stories in the local and state newspapers. These were headlines in the *Seattle Star* during hearings to determine the fate of Japanese immigrants in Washington State in 1920.

"WILL YOU HELP TO KEEP THIS A WHITE MAN'S COUNTRY?"

"JAPS PLANS MENACE WHITE CIVILIZATION"

"Japanese plans for expansion at the expense of the white race are a deeper menace to Caucasian civilization than were ever the dreams of Pan-German imperialists"

In the 1920 version of fake news, testifiers at the hearings repeated lies about the Japanese and weird ideas about racial purity that were then amplified by newspapers across the state. A well-organized American Legion, the Veterans of Foreign Wars and the Anti-Japanese League perpetuated the apocryphal threat of the Yellow Peril. Then the Grange took up the cause. Anti-alien laws passed in Washington State were modeled on those of California, which in turn had been promoted by influential Southern whites who had settled in the West after the Civil War.

Racist organizations gained influence after World War I. In the Red Scare of 1917-20 nativism swept the whole country. During that time Alien and Sedition laws were used to deport hundreds of immigrants deemed by the government to be radicals, the anarchist Emma Goldman among them. In the Yakima Valley anti-immigrant sentiment reached a peak in the 1920s and 30s. I was shocked to learn that the KKK held a rally in 1924 which drew 40,000 people to a field outside the town. A thousand robed KKK members marched in the parade.

The big industry in Yakima was, and still is, agriculture. My mother's family worked in the apple orchards, hop fields and fruit packing plants. Farmers welcomed migrant laborers during harvest season and when labor was scarce. But when the economic cycle moved from boom to bust, these workers were targets of violence, forced removal and alien restriction laws. American workers who saw their jobs being taken by immigrants who would work for less were some of the worst perpetrators of nativist violence.

In 1938, 200 men set upon Blacks in Wapato, beating them and setting fire to one of their houses. Filipinos and unionists also became targets of harassment. In 1933, the Industrial Workers of the World (the Wobblies) led a strike for higher wages of white migrant farmworkers that was put down by orchardists with pipes, clubs and bats. Then the strikers were marched five miles to a stockade that had been constructed in the middle of downtown Yakima. Some of those arrested were jailed for six months, and the stockade stayed up as a deterrent for a decade.

In the Yakima of my mother's youth you could not escape the dominant paradigm. But by the time I was growing up in the 1950s and 60s, my generation was ignorant of this history. I grew up near the Congdon orchard where the 1933 "Battle of Congdon Castle" took place. The owner's summerhouse mansion was called Congdon Castle and we kids thought it was haunted. No one really lived there except caretakers. The wealthy owners had always lived in another state. A footnote here: my Swedish carpenter uncle was a builder of the castle whose architecture was reminiscent of Medieval Europe.

Our family often visited Fort Simcoe, the restored Army fort on the Yakama reservation, but I never learned about the Indian Wars as a child. Indians and revolution were scrubbed from our textbooks and xenophobia persisted. My brother Don remembers as a freshman in high school in 1967 defending the rights of Native Americans in history class. The popular teacher launched into a diatribe against him in front of the whole class. She said Indians had an inferior culture and deserved to be conquered. She said they were dirty, barbaric and uncivilized. She believed it was the right of a superior culture to war against them and subjugate them. This was the inevitable march of history, she said.

In Yakima the xenophobes scorned anyone not of the "white race." The irony was that these invading whites had themselves displaced indigenous people and it's difficult to understand how they failed to see this giant contradiction. The trick, of course, was to make them subhuman.

The advantage my family had is that they were, in the language of the American Legion, of the "white race." The white supremacists in Yakima and elsewhere were able to successfully construct a racial identity, the "white race," made from hundreds of diverse cultures, people who spoke different languages and dialects, people who had themselves been the victims of oppression, as a way to successfully divide the population.

In Yakima white was all right as long as you didn't upset the status quo. Whiteness didn't always save you. As a method of exclusion, the definition of white has changed significantly over the course of our history. Europeans not considered white at some point in American history include Italians, Greeks, Spaniards, Irish, Scandinavians, Germans, Finns, Russians, French, and Jews.

My grandparents had a strong immigrant identity and they can't have felt completely safe. Family lore tells of my grandfather Ben enduring taunts for his foreign accent from students at Yakima High School where he taught commercial arts. Mom told me she remembered her father's troubled reaction to the execution of Sacco and Vanzetti, Italian immigrants whose incarceration lasted from 1920 to 1927. She was 14 years old when they were executed by the US government. Her Norwegian father took the side of the immigrants, who most agreed had been falsely accused.

The Irish side of my family immigrated just before the onset of the potato famine of the 1840s, what the Irish call the starvation because the crops they grew and harvested were shipped to their English overlords, leaving them with nothing to eat. In his book, *Irish on the Inside*, Tom Hayden posits that Irish immigrants had more in common with Blacks and slaves than the white rulers who starved and oppressed them. Before epigenetics became a thing, Hayden made the case that we have all been affected by the plight of our ancestors. "That the Irish are white and European cannot erase the experience of our having been invaded, occupied, starved, colonized and forced out of our homeland," he wrote.

Hayden wanted to break the assimilationist mold among Irish Americans. "If Irish Americans identify with the 10 percent of the world which is white, Anglo American and consumes half the global resources, we have chosen the wrong side of history and justice. We will become the inhabitants of the Big House ourselves, looking down on the natives we used to be. We will become our nightmare without a chance of awakening from its grip."

One white Yakiman who tried to choose the right side of history and justice was William O. Douglas. My mother was one of the few locals who admired him. She shared his politics, which were shaped by class. He grew up fatherless and poor. When discussing how his personal experiences influenced his view of the law, Douglas said, "I worked among the very, very poor, the migrant laborers, the Chicanos and the IWWs who I saw being shot at by the police. I saw cruelty and hardness, and my impulse was to be a force in other developments in the law."

The anti-communist John Birch Society smeared Douglas as "the only known Communist in Yakima County." He was no Communist but he did defend the concept of revolution in a 1969 screed. He is famously quoted in *Points of Rebellion*: "We must realize that today's Establishment is the new George III. Whether it will continue to adhere to his tactics, we do not know. If it does, the redress, honored in tradition, is also revolution." He survived four impeachment attempts.

When I asked my civil rights lawyer friend Judy Kurtz about Douglas she said, "Legal standing for trees!" He was famous for defending nature and the environment, often in dissenting opinions. She added, "I wish he was still on the court. Dear god, help us now."

Douglas called Yakima his "Shangri-La." He loved the orchards and the nearby Cascade Mountains. He returned often to our hometown and Mom and I ran into him and his wife Cathy in the 1970s. We had decided to splurge on lunch at the Larson Building, the town's only high-rise, an elegant Art Deco architectural gem built in 1931. Mom spotted them as we walked into the lobby. "Justice Douglas, Justice Douglas," my mother entreated as she ran up to him. He graciously remembered her father.

My grandfather's membership in the Democratic Party came at a high price. He was let go from his teaching job at the nadir of the Depression in 1932. After that the family, with four young daughters, struggled to survive.

The wartime internment of Japanese did not happen in a vacuum. Finally, after decades of domestic terrorism, the American

Legion and its ilk got their way. In June 1942, 1,061 Japanese were evacuated from the Valley, sent by rail to a processing center at the Portland livestock grounds, and then incarcerated at Heart Mountain, Wyoming for the remainder of the war—800 miles from home. Only a few resettled in the Yakima Valley.

Now, a century after my grandparents immigrated, in a time when, once again, militias form to "protect" the white race from foreigners, we can look to our own history for insight. One of my heroes, the labor organizer Sister Addie Wyatt said, "If you don't know where you come from, you don't know where you're going." This is where we come from. I fervently hope it is not where we're going. I'm so glad people like immigrants and Americans of color, the Wobblies, my grandfather and William O. Douglas found the will to resist.

Tradeswomen Fiction: Stories of Working While Female

Sweetheart

I was doing pretty good on this new job. See, they didn't want to hire me. Said four foot eleven was too short to be a mechanic. The trucks are put up to a certain height they said and I wasn't tall enough to reach them. But after I complained to Fair Employment, they decided it was okay for me to use a ladder.

So here I am on my little ladder under a diesel changing the oil. The roll-up doors on the garage are all open so I'm kind of on display. And I'm the first woman so I'm a curiosity. They all make detours past the maintenance shop just to see me on my ladder. As if I was a two-headed snake or something. Strange how their minds work. Or they'll come in with some "problem" just to get a look at me. Sometimes they'll walk past and make comments, sort of muttered under their breath, but I know they mean for me to hear. I try not to, though. I concentrate on my work and try to ignore them. They're chicken, anyhow. I say, you don't like somebody, you just tell 'em to their face. I'd have more respect for them if they talked right to me.

One time I thought I heard the word bitch but when I turned around the guy was gone, out the door. Now I don't know if it really happened or if I was just paranoid. I decided it doesn't really matter one way or the other, whether I hear it or not. They're trying to get my goat. They're letting me know they don't want me. Well, you do that to me, it's like waving red in front of a bull. No way am I quittin' now. The more they bug me, the harder I dig my heels in. Besides, this is the best money I ever made. Beats waitressing any day.

So anyhow, I'm standing there under this truck and I hear from across the yard kinda sing-song but loud, "Hey, sweetheart, how ya doin' today?" I squint out into the sun and see this big old red-faced guy waving his arms at me. His belly looks like a hundred-pound sack of flour slung over a farmer's shoulder. His waving arms cause the sack of flour to jiggle and expose a rim of pink flesh above his belt. His head looks like an engine block, hair shaved into a military flat top. He must be a teamster, I think. No neck.

I gotta admit my first impulse was to laugh at this fool. Next I wanted to punch his lights out. Now I know some women don't mind being called sweetheart or honey or any of those sugar-coated names. Men will tell you women think it's a compliment—especially older women. Then they look at me as if I should understand. You know, I'm not that old, but it seems like I hate this name calling more the older I get.

I decided if I ignored this joker maybe he'd get the point and leave me alone. Wouldn't you know, that tactic only encouraged him. Every time he'd see me, he'd yell "Heeeeey sweeeeetheart" at the top of his lungs so everyone could hear. One day he came right up and introduced himself, friendly as can be. "Hey," he says, holding out a grimy hand, "I'm Harry. Harry the Hunk they call me." I'm like, is he kidding? Harry the Hunk! Is he putting himself down? I had to hide a smile. I wanted to appear serious, intimidating if possible.

My name's Bev," I scowled, "and I'd appreciate it if you'd call me that."

"Okay, sweetheart," he leered, and walked away.

Well you can imagine, that got my dander up. I fumed about that all week. It got so every night I'd be beating up Harry the Hunk in my dreams.

Now I've never been one to criticize any woman for how she chooses to survive in a job. We each pick our own battles. God knows you can't take on every one that comes along. You'd be wrung out like a dish rag at the end of every day. Some insults are better ignored, but some if they were water wouldn't even slide off a duck's back. So I determined to take on Harry the Hunk or my mind would never be set at ease as long as I worked on this job.

By this time I've been on the job awhile and I've gotten to know the crew of mechanics in my shop. They turned out to be a pretty good group after all. Dave struck me as a Hell's Angels type at first glance. Kinda scruffy, his beard half grown out. Yeah, I know that's in style now, but believe me on him it looks scruffy. Skinny as a cotter pin and at least six three. Drives a Harley. He's the first to talk to me. "Don't let 'em get to you," he says. "I know what you're going through. My wife's a sheet metal apprentice."

I'm like, no kidding. We were instant friends.

Well, that broke the ice. The others might have been a little jealous of Dave, or they might have decided I'm no more different from any of them than they are from each other. Two are immigrants, from Ireland and El Salvador. The rest are Blacks, whites, and Chicanos.

We circled around each other for a while, testing limits. I had to tell one or two not to call me girl or honey. Had to thank them for their offers of help, but let them know I've got two arms, I can carry things just like taller people. Maybe better, 'cause I'm closer to the ground.

I did almost get into a scrape with the shop boss, Fernando, a very proper Catholic gentleman who let me know in so many words he thinks women belong at home and not in a garage earning a man's wage. In his world women don't leave their children to go to work, they don't wear pants, and they don't swear.

Now all my friends know I can cuss a streak as blue as any

sailor. I let the guys know swearing doesn't bother me at all. So I'm starting to feel real comfortable in the shop, and one day I'm shooting the breeze with Fernando trying to tell him I deserve a good job, I've got three kids to support just like him, when I guess I let a four-letter word drop. Well, he gets this look on his face all kind of furrowed and scrunched. I swear the corners of his mouth drooped more than his mustache. His eyes turned into little black ball bearings under his bushy brows. Then he draws himself up and says, "Dear, I don't see any reason to use that word."

Course I know this is not true since I hear the guys say it all the time. What he means is he has a different standard for women and men. Well, you know I'll fight for a lot of things, but my right to swear at work is not first on my list. So I say, "Okay, Fernando, I'll make a deal with you. I'll never swear in front of you again, if from now on you call me Bev instead of dear." He thinks this is an honorable agreement, and we even shake on it, though I suspect he doesn't think women ought to shake either.

Turns out Fernando took me seriously. Called me by my name from then on. I've kept my part too, ever since, and our truce stood me in good stead in my ongoing battle with Harry the Hunk. Fernando could see what was going on. So, after that, when Harry would come through the shop, before he could even get his big mouth open, Fernando would yell at him, "Heeeeey Sweeeeetheart!"

This should have been enough to make any grown man blush, but Harry just took it in his stride. He'd smile sheepishly and go about his business. But he wouldn't stop calling me sweetheart.

Then one day I hear Harry lay the same trip on Dave. "Hey, hippie," he says, "when are you gonna get a haircut?" Harry's smiling the whole time but I can tell Dave doesn't think it's funny. Dave just keeps his mouth shut and concentrates on his brake job.

Harry keeps smiling at me, too, and I start to figure out the only way he knows how to be friendly is harassing people. But I decide I don't care. I never liked being called names and I'm not gonna get used to it. If he wants to make friends he's got to at least learn my name.

One day I put it to him. "Harry," I say, "why do you keep calling me sweetheart when you know I hate it?

"You hate it?" he says. "But I call my wife sweetheart and she loves it."

"Harry, I'm not your wife. I'm your coworker, Bev. I'm not your sweetheart." Now I'm thinking this guy is thick. He really doesn't get it. This is gonna be harder than I thought.

A while later he brings in his truck for emergency work and I'm the only mechanic available. "Come on," he says, "hop to it, sweetheart. I gotta get this baby back on the road."

"Harry," I say, "either you never learned the mechanics' law or you forgot it."

"Mechanics' law, what's that?" he says.

"Very basic," I say. "The law says you treat your mechanic right, you got a smooth-running truck. Treat your mechanic bad and your truck never gets out of the shop. Harry, if you don't stop calling me sweetheart, you could be a permanent pedestrian."

"Okay, okay," he says, "if it means that much to you. I really need my truck...Bev."

I could see his mouth had great difficulty forming the word, but it was a start. After that, he seemed to try harder. He'd bolt into the shop in his usual back slapping, shoulder punching way and yell, "Hey, Swee...Bev." This was a great improvement, and I told myself I'd made progress, but Harry seemed to be having a hard time making the transition. I couldn't tell whether his harassment had taken a new form or his mind just wasn't making the connection.

Now that we're "friends" Harry thinks he can take new liberties. One day he lopes over, yells, "Hey, Swee...Bev," and wraps his arms around me in a bear hug. I duck, but not soon enough, and he gets me in a headlock.

I growl at him, "Harry, what are you doing?"

He looks hurt. "Just saying hello."

So after that whenever he sees me he holds his arms outstretched as if to hug me and gets this sad teddy bear lost puppy look on his face. God, I think, I've created a monster.

"*Jeez*, Harry, go hug an I-beam."

Harry finally learns to say my name without having to stop and think every time. Natural as can be, he comes in and says, "Hey, Bev, how ya doin'?" We chit chat about our kids. I ask him how his wife puts up with him. He tells me she's really a liberated woman. I start to actually like the guy, but as soon as I let him know that, he thinks all the rules are off. He thinks he can call me whatever he wants and I'll go along with the program.

I run into him as I'm hurrying across the yard on my way back from lunch break. "Hey, sweetheart," he grins, arms outstretched as he walks toward me. I can see if I keep walking I'll head right into his grasp, so I have to stop and move sideways like a crab to avoid him.

When this happens, I frown, cross my arms, look him straight in the eye and say something like, "Harry, go drive your truck off a cliff." I'm trying to let him know I'm not playing, but to him this is the game.

One day he walks into the shop with a woman. I should say Amazon. This woman's gotta be six feet tall. Built like a linebacker. Her skin is the color of Columbian coffee. Her black hair is knotted up under a red kerchief and she's dressed in work clothes and boots, so she's got to be working here. Another woman in the yard! I'm thinking, who is she, what does she do? when Harry brings her right over to introduce me.

"Sweetheart," he booms, "I want you to meet my new partner, Pam." He's grinning so wide, his teeth take up half his face.

Now people say I'm easygoing. I'm known for my high boiling point. But I swear when Harry says this I feel like an engine overheating. Smoke must be coming out of my ears. I have to hold my arms next to my sides to keep from strangling him, and I start yelling all the words I promised Fernando I wouldn't.

"Aww, come on," he whines, "I was only kidding."

"Harry," I hiss, "don't call me sweetheart. It's not funny, it was never funny, and it's never gonna be funny."

When he turns around and walks out of the shop I hope I never see the jerk again. I also hope Pam doesn't think I'm a total nutcase. I do want to talk to her. But a little while later Harry slinks back in, alone this time, and stands beyond punching distance from me, head hanging, and says in a low voice, "Bev, I'm really sorry. You know I didn't mean to make you mad. I was just showing off to my partner. I promise, I'll never do it again."

"Right," I say, and jerk my socket wrench so hard I take a slice of skin off my thumb knuckle when it hits the block.

By this time I don't trust Harry the Hunk for a minute, and I tell myself I'm never gonna get set up again. So I just try to avoid him and be real busy whenever he comes by. He still acts friendly and says hi and I try to be civil. He always calls me Bev, still yelling as loud as ever. And because I'm not a person who can hold a grudge, I loosen up and let my defenses down some. Pretty soon we're back to our old routine. But he's never called me sweetheart since.

One day he stops by and gives me a hand with a generator I'm trying to move. "Thanks," I say. "I don't care what they say about you. You're okay."

"Hey, Bev," he grins, "all that work paid off. I turned out okay, huh."

"Yeah, Harry," I say, "and it only took me five years."

Bathroom Conversation

One afternoon a lawyer went to the restroom and found an electrician on a ladder fixing the light in the middle of the room.

The lawyer was startled. "Oh, excuse me," she said, and started to leave.

"It's okay," said the electrician. "Really. I'm one of you."

"You're a woman!" said the lawyer. "I'm sorry. I thought you were a man."

"I know," she laughed. "It happens all the time. Actually, you were very polite. The sight of me has caused women to run screaming from bathrooms. They've insisted that I must have misread the sign on the door. Sometimes, even after they've heard my voice, they refuse to believe I'm a woman."

"That's incredible. You don't sound like a man. And now that I look at you, you don't really look like a man, either. It must be hard to have to explain yourself so often. Excuse me, but I really did come in here to use the toilet."

The lawyer locked herself in a stall, and the electrician wondered if she was still a little suspicious.

"You don't see many women electricians," said the lawyer from the stall. "Does it bother you when people mistake you for a man?"

The electrician put a screwdriver back in her tool belt and reached for a pair of sidecutters. "Not usually," she said, carefully disconnecting wires, "I get a kick out of confusing people's stereotypes. But it also happens to me when I'm not at work. I wear jeans a lot."

"And you do have short hair."

"That's mainly because it's so much easier. Just like jeans and

168

tennis shoes. It seems to me that looking feminine takes work. Unisex is natural. Still, I do object to being seen as a man. It's made me realize how quick we are to categorize people. I wish we could see each other first as human beings, and gender wasn't so important."

The electrician heard the toilet flushing and watched out of the corner of her eye as the lawyer smoothed her skirt and walked to the mirror. The smart navy suit was probably Brooks Brothers. A Dianne Feinstein bow at the collar provided a feminine touch. The lawyer brushed her shoulder-length auburn hair into a smooth pageboy. The electrician thought she did appear both attractive and businesslike.

"If it creates an identity crisis, why *do* you dress like a man?" said the lawyer.

"You mean why do I insist on wearing the kind of clothes I like and being comfortable? It's not *my* problem that people sometimes think I'm a man, and it *doesn't* create an identity crisis. I certainly don't aspire to be male."

"People need to know your gender," said the lawyer, and touched up her lipstick, a muted shade of red.

"I can't deny that the ability to pass as a man is sometimes advantageous," said the electrician. "I've never been raped, which I count mostly as luck. But it doesn't hurt to be seen as a man on the street. Believe me, people treat you very differently."

"Really," said the lawyer. "How?"

"Mostly they just leave you alone, which I generally prefer to catcalls and verbal harassment. I feel much safer. Besides, I can use the men's bathroom at the movies and public events."

"You're kidding."

"Haven't you noticed?" the electrician laughed. "The lines are much shorter."

The lawyer slouched into the overstuffed Naugahyde chair in the corner, kicked off her pumps, and pulled a pack of cigarettes from her purse. She lit one with a sigh of pleasure as she appraised the woman on the ladder. Particles of plaster and concrete formed a snow-like mantle on the electrician's dark hair. She wore clunky, scuffed, thick-soled work boots and stained faded denim jeans. The sleeves of her flannel shirt were rolled up, revealing ropey forearm muscles. Her strong hands moved with quick assurance between the ceiling and the tool pouch belted around her hips.

"Must you smoke?" said the electrician. "It's worse up here, you know."

"Sorry, but I have to get my tobacco fix. This is my only refuge. It's against the law in the office now."

The electrician frowned and squinted at the old light fixture in her hands, and climbed down, setting it carefully on the floor.

"Smoking cigarettes seems like a rather unladylike habit if you ask me," she teased.

The lawyer took a long drag. "Funny," she said, "I used to think it gave me more power among my male colleagues. Now, of course, I wish I'd never started." She opened one of the dingy windows and held her cigarette near the opening. "Maybe this will help."

"Thanks," said the electrician, noting that the influx of cold air was pushing the smoke into the room rather than out, and thinking to herself that the thought counts for something.

"Do you think wearing a skirt gives you more power on the job?" asked the electrician.

The lawyer took a long drag and exhaled. "Yes. There is a kind of power I feel when men are attracted to me. They want something I have the power to give and withhold. It's one of the few ways women get noticed—a bit of leg and a shapely figure. Of course, in the business world you can't be too sexy or you aren't taken seriously. But it's still hard for us out there, and I take advantage of whatever I can."

The electrician chose a drill bit, tightened the chuck on her hammer drill, ascended the ladder, pulled on her safety glasses, and drilled a hole in the ceiling. Whucka, whucka, whucka, whucka. "What about the heels?" she said. "Be honest."

"Okay, I admit we have to wear heels to get ahead. You can tell which women in the company are ambitious by the height of their heels. Three-inch spikes every day would be overdoing it, of course. But I believe *some* heel is required for advancement. Women in flats have opted out of the race for promotions, for whatever reasons. They like their jobs and want to stay where they are..."

"Or they've decided not to compromise their integrity." Whucka, whucka, whucka, whucka.

"Or they just want to be comfortable for eight hours."

The electrician descended the ladder to look for lead anchors to pound into the holes in the ceiling. "What about you?" she asked.

"The one-inch heels? My own little compromise. I can be relatively comfortable and still protect my chances for promotion. I do have tennis shoes stashed in a bottom drawer of my desk."

"Incredible," said the electrician, hoisting a new fixture up the ladder.

The lawyer frowned and lit another cigarette. "There must be some parallel in your trade."

"Not really," she said, pounding in the anchors. "You're either an apprentice or journeyworker—you know, skilled. There *are* no promotions. But dressing like a construction worker doesn't exempt me from passes and harassment—just the opposite. Maybe my freedom to wear these clothes threatens men somehow."

"Or maybe it's your freedom to do their job."

Ceiling dust formed a cloud around the electrician as she jockeyed the light fixture into place. "They comment on my body a lot," she puffed. "You know, 'Haven't you lost or gained weight? Are you pregnant? I bet you'd look great in a slinky dress.' Things like that. What's funny is no matter how hard I try to blend into the woodwork, I stick out." She set the fixture down on the ladder, put a hand over one eye, and made her way down slowly.

"What's the matter?" asked the lawyer.

"It's my own fault for not using my safety glasses. I got something in my eye." The electrician peered at herself in the mirror.

"Can I help?" asked the lawyer, politely, eyeing the soiled work clothes and wondering if her suit would suffer from close contact.

"No, it's okay. It happens all the time," said the electrician, cupping her water-filled hand to her eye. "Actually, this is a gravy job. This bathroom is heaven. On construction sites we use outhouses. They smell, and they're filled with graffiti—mostly about women. Well, you can imagine." The lawyer did try to imagine, and was suddenly very grateful for her own working conditions.

"There, I think I got it," said the electrician. She made her way back up the ladder. "This job is warm and dry, and the crawl spaces are roomy. There's no asbestos that I know of. Best of all, I'm working by myself."

The door creaked open and another woman hurried in. "Oh, excuse me," she said, bewildered.

"It's okay," said the lawyer. "She's one of us."

Graffiti War

"I saw what they wrote about you in the outhouse," says Judy.

"I know, but I'm not gonna let those pinche pendejos get to me." Dolores throws her hard hat on the plywood and runs a hand through long black curly hair. She takes gum from her mouth and throws it out onto the gravel driveway.

"We can't let them say those things." When Judy's hard hat comes off, it leaves a sweaty indentation all around her head of short brown hair. She wipes a sweatshirt sleeve across her forehead.

Dolores and Judy eat lunch together every day. Every day that they're both on the job. When Dolores isn't sick. She's been sick a lot lately. Her stomach acts up, she can't eat, and she's already skinny.

Judy brings her lunch in a black plastic lunch box: tuna fish sandwich, apple, cookies, orange juice in a thermos. Dolores usually can't get it together and picks up a carton of milk and a sagging burrito wrapped in plastic from the roach coach.

They sit on a stack of plywood forms at the edge of the jobsite. It is a rainy spring, and here they are protected from the weather by the concrete floor above, but they can still see the street three floors below. Eight more floors have yet to be formed and poured. Exterior walls won't be in place for months. Here the women talk for a short half hour until the whistle summons them back to work.

"Who cares what those cabrones think." Dolores scowls, waving her plastic burrito in the air. "They don't bother me. Besides, they've done worse. They pissed in my toolbox. They gave me the crummiest, dirtiest jobs, hoping I'd quit. They call me names behind my back and to my face."

"But this is too much," says Judy. "It's bad enough having to use those smelly shitters without seeing your name all over the walls."

"I take care of myself, don't you worry." Dolores throws off her yellow raincoat and stretches out on the plywood, hands behind her head. Her thin mouth twists into a smirk. "I went after one of them with a hammer today."

Judy swallows a bite of sandwich and sits up. "Are you okay? What happened?"

"You know the guy. They call him Redneck. The name fits. Tried to take my hammer away. Said he was gonna show me how to pound a nail right. I said I'd pound his ass first, and I went after him. Would have hit him, too, but he got out of my way real fast. I could have killed that pendejo." Dolores eyes the burrito with disgust. "Now I'm still so pissed off I can't eat."

Dolores is a second-year apprentice carpenter. Seventy percent, which means she now makes seventy percent of a journeyworker's wage. She decided to be a carpenter when she got tired of waiting on her boss and running for coffee. Now she runs for 50-pound boxes of nails and four-by-fours, but for twice the pay.

"Call the union," says Judy. "They're supposed to protect you from harassment."

Dolores sneers. "Come on. My union doesn't want me here any more than the contractor. I heard about a woman who called the business agent. He came down to the job and told her in front of her whole crew she should stop making trouble. He said everything was fine before she got there. I don't need that."

"If they didn't want you, how did you get in the union?"

"Same as you, chica. Affirmative action. You know there's federal money on this job. They have goals for women and minorities.

They can count me twice and they do. There's lots of Mexicans on this job, but they're all laborers. I'm the only Mexican carpenter here and the only woman working for this contractor. They hate us, mujer, and that's never gonna change."

"They're not all bad," says Judy. "I like my tool partner. But whoever wrote that graffiti has gone too far. They could start writing about me next. As far as I'm concerned, this is war."

Judy is a first-year plumber apprentice. A stocky, athletic woman, she fidgeted and daydreamed through years of office work, trying to imagine a job that could be like a playing field, full of physical challenge, activity and teamwork. A job devoid of paper and typewriters. After much cajoling, Judy convinced her brother, who is a plumber, to help her get into the union.

Her partner's trade name is Captain America, a tall, copper-skinned man with a sparse beard and one pierced ear. Sometimes he wears a skull and crossbones earring, sometimes a green crystal. Once Judy asked him about his ethnic background and he told her about a Spanish conquistador and an Indian princess. She thinks she believes him. Anyway, it made a good story.

"I need to think of a comeback," she says after lunch. "Did you see what they wrote about Dolores in that outhouse over there? It says THE LITTLE WOMAN CARPENTER TAKES IT IN THE ASS. Then they added other body parts."

Captain shades his eyes. He doesn't want responsibility for this.

"I need a comeback," she says, but he just shakes his head and bears down on a coupling with his pipe wrench.

That night Judy calls her carpenter friend Cheryl. "I need a comeback," she says.

"At least they wrote WOMAN," says Cheryl. "Maybe we should

consider this progress."

"Come on," says Judy. "I need your help."

"I've got it," says Cheryl. "THE LITTLE WOMAN CARPENTER TAKES IT WITH HER SKILSAW."

Judy howls. "Perfect!"

The next day she tells her comeback to Captain, who responds with a pained look and a hand over his genitals.

"It works," she smiles. But they are running pipe in another part of the building and she doesn't get a chance to change the graffiti. Later, armed with a black marker, she goes back to look for the outhouse.

Judy has perfected a method of using outhouses. After trying the door to check for another occupant, you drop your tools outside the door. Then you get ready to drop your overalls. Everything must be accomplished fast, and as much as possible outside the door because of the stench. Great care must be taken to avoid any reason to stay in the outhouse any longer than necessary. You take a deep breath before you enter, then once inside, breathe shallowly or into your shirt sleeve. Overalls are the tricky part. If you casually let them drop, then all the pencils and little tools you've stored in the front pocket fall out onto the grungy floor. Someday, she thinks, designers of overalls will consider this problem. Those little slits in the front will be replaced by—what?—something for women.

Once settled on the damp seat, Judy looks at the wall where she saw the graffiti. Nothing is there except some unintelligible gibberish. She can pick out the word DAGO, but nothing else. What's happened? Graffiti is never cleaned off. It just gets added to and marked out until the job ends. Then Judy remembers how the fiberglass toilets get cleaned every two weeks. The big crane at the center of the job lifts each one over to a "honey wagon" where it gets pumped out. Then the crane sets it down again, somewhere on the jobsite. That outhouse with the graffiti about Dolores could be anywhere now, and the job is too big to run all over looking for it. The crew boss expects you to be in a particular spot working, or at least moving fast looking busy.

Judy scans this shack's bright blue interior. Several disembodied sets of balls and cocks decorate the walls. The penises are in various states of erection. Sometimes there is an accompanying label designating some particular construction worker, usually without a last name. On the door is a large drawing of the lower half of a woman lying spread-eagled, knees up. It is well rendered by an obviously practiced artist. Before she leaves, she wipes out the picture with her black marker. Then she draws mouths underneath the penises and makes the balls into eyes.

"I've failed," Judy tells Dolores at lunch. "I waited too long and they've moved the outhouse. Now I can't find it."

The two women settle onto their plywood perch. On the street below, office workers scurry about, umbrellas shielding them from the ceaseless drizzle. The usual construction sounds of compressor engines, electric tool motors and constant hammering have been replaced by city street noise.

Judy stops rummaging through plastic containers and bags in her lunch box and says thoughtfully, "Dolores, those pictures they draw. I know they'd draw them whether we were here or not, but why do you suppose they do it? Whenever I see that stuff, I feel like an anthropologist studying creatures from outer space. If construction workers were all women, would we draw tits and cunts in the shitters?"

"The cabrones just have to inflate the size of their egos." Dolores looks like she could fight them all. Her small frame radiates hostile energy, chin stuck out, fists clenched. "First thing this morning the guy they call Big Bob tried to tell me a Mexican joke. I can't believe it. I'm supposed to laugh. When I didn't, he tells me Pepe always laughs, and in fact Pepe tells funnier Mexican jokes than the white boys. I said to just don't ever tell them around me and if I heard any good white boy jokes, I'd return the favor."

"I'm gonna keep looking for that outhouse," says Judy. "What's wrong? Aren't you eating?"

"Can't, chica. My stomach is sick. Since I got this job, nothing stays down."

"What are you doing about it?"

"I saw a doctor. They did tests, but they say there's nothing wrong. Then they ask me do I have any stress in my life. I say not unless you count walking into a war zone every morning. Chica, I don't want to quit, but I think this job is making me sick."

Judy doesn't see Dolores after that. Rumor has it she was laid off for absenteeism. Weeks later, Judy finds the outhouse with the old graffiti. Underneath is written LAY OFF. YOU MIGHT BE INSULTING ONE OF MY RELATIVES. It was signed CAPTAIN AMERICA.

Deck Job

The day we were to do the estimate on Catherine Moore's house, my horoscope said I would meet a romantic partner. I do not believe in astrology. Still, I do read my horoscope daily. There, in the Chronicle, is something to gauge one's life by, something to provide optimism or set conditions when there is no other frame of reference. Perhaps reading a fatalistic account of one's day might also create a mindset. Do we seek to accomplish what fate sets forth? In any case, I remain a skeptic.

My lover and I were a bit late. Everyone says contractors are notoriously undependable, but if they only knew the problems we have, answering calls from clients at all hours, usually with emergencies that they say can't wait. You just can't keep them all happy. And projects inevitably take longer than expected. That day Sandy had been putting finishing touches on a stair job so we could collect the final payment, which would keep other checks from bouncing.

Catherine Moore's house was a well-maintained Victorian complete with gingerbread and a three-tone paint job. I imagined its owner to be an established professional. We were greeted by a large, gray-haired fortyish woman dressed in Katherine Hepburn slacks and a tailored shirt. She shook both our hands, and I could tell she worked at a white-collar job if she worked at all. But there was no hint of condescension in her warm greeting.

"You must be Sandy and Jill. Please come in."

Sandy introduced herself as the carpenter and me as the jill-of-all-trades. I'm an electrician first, but I'm also proficient at simple plumbing, and I swing a mean hammer when I have to.

"You have the perfect combination of talents," said Catherine Moore. Her speech was charming, aristocratic, and there was something about her mouth that fascinated me. I waited for her to speak again.

We were led into a spacious, tastefully decorated room. "You see, where this door is now," she addressed Sandy, "I want double French doors to open onto a deck with stairs leading into the garden." I watched, captivated, as she explained the addition. Her full lips fit so precisely over the large perfect teeth with each clipped syllable. Her movements were so self-assured, so all-encompassing. I found myself wishing to be clasped in those arms, smothered by those lips.

Could she cast this spell on everyone, I wondered. I tried to catch Sandy's eye, but she seemed intent and businesslike. By the time we got around to talking about electrical and plumbing, all my energy was concentrated on maintaining my composure. I was to install new track lighting in the kitchen, add an electrical outlet and replace the kitchen faucet and the trap under the sink.

The contract was drawn up and signed that day. If there had been another estimate, no mention was made of it. Catherine Moore wanted us to start as soon as possible.

In the truck, I fished for Sandy's reaction. "Isn't she an interesting woman!"

Sandy's sidelong glance told me she understood more than I'd intended. "You have a crush on her?" she teased.

"Well, yes, a little," I admitted, resolving silently to suppress it. I wouldn't do anything to damage our monogamous relationship. The understanding—no other women—had been very clear from the beginning, two years before. I had been the jealous one and it was Sandy, who, at my ultimatum, had given up her other lover. I knew my commitment would pass this test.

The job progressed smoothly. I helped Sandy build the deck structure outside, then while she finished the deck I moved my electrical and plumbing tools into the kitchen.

Catherine Moore, it turned out, was a self-employed accountant. She spent most of her day in her office, a room that had once been the Victorian's parlor, but she would read the morning paper over coffee in the kitchen and would chat with me while I worked.

We developed a routine. She would make me a pot of tea (I'm not a coffee drinker), then sit down and sort of read the news to me, adding her own running commentary. She read our horoscopes with such obvious pleasure that I began to suspect the attraction was mutual. These were particularly romantic times for both of us, astrologically, and more than once I hid my reddening face pretending to be engrossed in some construction problem.

"It's completely bogus, of course," I said.

"Perhaps," she said, and a playful smile crinkled the corners of her eyes. "But perhaps we can't afford to overlook it."

My infatuation refused to wear off. Instead it intensified with new knowledge of Catherine Moore. She was at once flirtatious and nurturing, wise and funny, powerful and defenseless. Even when my work took me elsewhere, I was acutely aware of her presence in the house. Intuition told me the excitement I felt could not be one-sided. Still, she gave no clear sign of her feelings. The uncertainty was maddening. But I was also confident in my well-practiced ability to hide my own feelings from public view, and sometimes even from myself. No one would guess at my obsession with this woman. And soon the job would be finished and my temptation gone.

One day, as I struggled with the trap under the sink, I felt her eyes on me. "Self-employed Scorpios fare well today," she read. "An older person plays a prominent role in your professional or personal life. Romance holds a delightful surprise."

She watched me silently. Swearing at the pipes and wriggling into a new position did nothing to ease my discomfort. Finally, I gave up and slid out from under the sink. She sat at the kitchen table, a peculiar expression on her face, almost tearful in its intensity. I said nothing, only wondering what trick my imagination had chosen to play on me. Then she came over to me, knelt down and put her hand on my cheek. "You have dirt on your face," she said.

The sheer force of exploding sexual tension propelled us into each other's arms, and I was aware of nothing beyond her lips until, looking up, I saw Sandy standing above us, open-mouthed, hammer in hand.

I am an actress in a lesbian soap opera, I thought, as she turned to go. "I'll just get my tools," she said. Surely this was only a line she had rehearsed. I didn't ask her to wait or come back. How would I have explained myself if she had?

Neither our surprise at being discovered nor my pain and guilt at hurting Sandy stilled the passion once it found its expression. That day, I moved into Catherine Moore's bed, leaving a message on the phone machine that I intended to indulge myself in this fantasy and that I hoped Sandy would still be there when I came home. We would have to work things out then, I thought, and resolved not to ponder the complications.

We've been lovers only a week, but I've confided to CM that in my 32 years I've never experienced such an intense emotional connection with another person. "When I put it into words it sounds silly," I say to her. "Do you know what I mean?"

"Yes," she says, and the core of me knows we understand each other perfectly without words. I turn on my side and look into her dark eyes and she examines my soul and I feel as if I know every part of her. Even shared, the vulnerability is terrifying. We kiss, and I am filled with wanting her, and we enter another world where nothing exists but the two of us, our senses are so totally focused on each other. There is a droning noise in my ears, in my head, and I wonder if this is what they mean when they say you hear bells ringing. But I am pulled and distracted by its menacing tone, and still it takes me a while to realize it is a chain saw I hear. Sandy's chain saw, I think, and I look at CM and we both sit up, staring stupidly as the deck falls gracefully away from the house and into the garden.

Mean Business

Two carpenters who had worked many years in isolation decided to become partners in a contracting business. While not good friends, they had known and worked with each other in a small-town community of activists where each was expected to do her part in the ongoing struggle for social justice. Wanda had been working tirelessly with a local group to stop the construction of a nuclear power plant nearby, while Deborah was part of a committee to end US intervention in Latin America. They were idealistic, energetic, and committed to the principle of struggle. At that time, in the 70s, the world seemed full of possibilities.

"I didn't think I would ever want to be a business owner," said Deb. "I've consciously chosen not to participate in the patriarchal capitalist system. The idea of self-sufficiency is appealing, though."

"But our business will embody the teachings of feminist theory, women working together in the spirit of true cooperation," explained Wanda, waving her arms about as she always did when enthusiastic.

"It's true, I've hated having to prove myself to men constantly, but I never wanted to be a boss," said Deb.

"Decision making will be collective, and all employees will benefit equally from the profits," promised Wanda.

Deb twisted a strand of long brown hair and frowned. "It's just that I know I'll hate having to tell people what to do. Especially women."

"But can't you see? It's a chance for us to live our politics. Skill sharing will be the number one priority. Each collective member will learn to perform all tasks. We can teach other women. Our

184

work will be meaningful!"

Deb suggested that they try doing one job together first. A friend of hers, an older woman, was looking for carpenters to remodel her bathroom. They went to look at the job together.

"We can expand the size of the room to here," said Wanda. "This is not a bearing wall, so it won't hurt to move it out."

Wow, thought Deb. She knows this trade. I'm working with another skilled woman! "The problem is there's not enough room for the door to swing. We could put in a pocket door," said Deb.

The two women looked at each other in a wave of recognition. They spoke the same language! Something happened then like love or liberation. The bathroom had become the blueprint for their dreams.

In this way Working Women Construction was born. From then on at the Matrix Café, tall, wiry Deb and wide, bosomy Wanda often made an odd couple hunkered over a table in concentrated conversation, discussing the pros and cons of post and beam construction or some equally uninviting topic. Friends learned not to join them.

While it was true that both Deb and Wanda were carpenters, their experiences in the craft were vastly different. Deb had completed a painful but comprehensive apprenticeship. After four years, she was still the only woman in her union local. Wanda, finding the union's doors closed to women, had scrounged work wherever she could find it, and had learned the trade by the seat of her pants and with the help of her handy father. By the time the union had grudgingly begun to admit women, Wanda had thumbed her nose at the chance to start at the bottom for half journey level pay. Wanda had estimated and bid jobs, haggled about money and learned to make decisions—right or wrong—without the help of a crew boss or experienced partner.

Deb had worked hard, to the point of exhaustion. She had swung a hammer until her hands were blistered and bleeding. She had performed feats of daring, walking on I-beams 40 feet above the ground. She had pushed herself to the limits of her emotional strength, enduring the harassment and outright hostility of co-workers and bosses. She had learned to do things right and as fast as possible in an eight-hour day with half an hour for lunch. Their very different backgrounds pleased both women at the outset and would, they agreed, enhance their shared store of knowledge.

The first few jobs were difficult but exhilarating. Deb and Wanda spent many of their evenings pricing materials, planning and estimating jobs, and budgeting their meager funds. They remodeled a kitchen and built a set of stairs. They repaired a termite infested foundation, digging by hand, jacking up the house with much trepidation and care.

By the time Working Women won a bid to build a house, Wanda and Deb were feeling more sure of themselves. They had bid low on the house mainly because they both wanted more than anything to build a whole house from foundation to roof. And this was no ordinary tract home. The plans showed a complex solar design with a multitude of roof angles, unusual room layout, and walls full of windows. Lumber was to be milled from the forested property.

"We'll have to work like hell to make this bid," said Wanda.

"My hammerin' arm's tuned up and ready to go," said Deb, who was more than a little worried herself. They signed the contract.

The foundation went in perfectly. Concrete work was the one part of the trade Deb knew a lot about. As an apprentice, she had built more forms than she cared to remember. At the end of the day finishing concrete, the women were exhausted and ecstatic. They could do this.

As the framing was begun, the women realized the need for more help. After much consternation and many interviews, they hired Joyce, an unemployed single mother who had no carpentry skills, but truly desired to learn a trade which might better help her support her two children. They agreed to pay her $4 an hour, as close to a starting apprentice wage as they thought they could afford. Joyce proved to be quite energetic, willing to learn, and full of questions.

Problems inevitably arose. The milled wood was from several different kinds of trees, and hence of different strengths requiring odd size beams. The windows arrived sized all wrong and had to be sent back. By the time the rafters were being framed, the only one of them getting paid regularly was Joyce.

"I know I said all workers would share equally in the profits, but how about the losses?" wondered Wanda.

"No way," said Deb, who was really a union carpenter at heart. "If we can't pay her, we lay her off."

Framing is a bust ass, go home and fall into bed kind of job, and as it proceeded Deb began to resent that Wanda spent so much time standing around thinking. In truth she was also jealous of Wanda's knowledge. She wanted to plan the roof framing, but she was completely intimidated by the thinking jobs she'd never been allowed to do as an apprentice.

"Hey, I want to learn that," she said to Wanda once, and Wanda had tried to explain, but Deb didn't get it and she felt even more stupid. Besides they were in a rush now, behind schedule. Better get back to framing, a job that Deb excelled at and loved. She could lose herself in it, stand back and admire her work at day's end.

There was one day they remembered as a high point—the day they invited all their women friends over to stand up the walls and hoist the big ceiling rafters in place. Photos from that day show a happy crew of strong, competent women who look like they could do anything they put their collective mind to.

Then the women went home and the small crew of three took up the outside sheathing. As Wanda took charge of layout, Deb's resentment grew, but one thing she had learned to do well was to tough it out without complaint and she resolved to do just that.

For her part, Wanda had been dealing with the house's owner, who was being a prick. He wouldn't bend on anything, especially money. They had agreed to build a house for their bid, and by god, they had a contract. It didn't matter that the architect's drawing was impossible to follow, or that lumber prices had gone up since the bid was made. They would have to eat it. Wanda would go home exhausted and not be able to sleep worrying about the house. Then she would arrive back at the work irritated as the burden of the house grew daily. Wanda began to wonder why all the responsibilities seemed to be falling on her shoulders.

Deb and Wanda decided to save money by not contracting out the roof, which then put them even more behind schedule. Teaching the trade to Joyce was taking far more time than either of them had imagined.

"Wanda, she's driving me crazy," confided Deb. "She asks so many questions, I just want to tell her to shut up. It takes me twice as long to do a job with her help than to just do it myself."

"I know," said Wanda, "but it's a good investment. Think what it'll be like when she's trained."

When the house was closed in they threw a party. It seemed that most of the work was finished, but they soon realized there were many more hurdles to jump. There was the prima donna electrician who could never seem to find time for their job. There was a plumbing contractor who thought that taking orders from women would endanger his manhood. There were the inspectors who really didn't believe women were capable of building a house and who wanted to argue about everything. With each encounter, the women ground their teeth and tried not to blame each other.

Their money ran out and Wanda started to feel that she was begging for credit whenever she went to the supply house. She had raised money for struggling nonprofits before, but this was different. It was too personal. She thought she understood how her parents must've felt during the Depression.

Deb carried around a stone in her chest, a sense of impending disaster. She felt like an animal before an earthquake. Something terrible seemed about to happen—something she had absolutely no control over. It was during the sheetrocking that Deb finally lost her patience.

"Hey," she yelled, "there's plenty of work here, if you need something to do. I'm sick of playing the apprentice to your foreman."

"Fuck you," Wanda yelled back. "I've been taking all the responsibility for this job."

Deb stepped over to where Wanda stood thinking and looked down at her. "That's because you never learned how to think and work at the same time. You haven't put in one honest day's work yet. If you hadn't stood around so much, we might have made the bid."

"You were the one who wanted to bid low to get this job." Wanda flushed. Her hands balled up into fists. Without thinking, in a gush of exasperation, she threw herself at Deb, knocking her to the ground.

Deb was startled. Wanda had pinned her down before she even realized what had happened, but as soon as that realization hit, a wave of anger washed out from her center and into her limbs. She pulled out of Wanda's grip in a rage and went for her throat.

"I'll kill you," she screamed, and in a flood of rage she felt she could do just that.

Joyce said later she saw the whole thing, and that no punches were thrown. The women just rolled around on the subfloor, she said. After she pulled them apart, Deb picked up her tools and stomped off the job.

Epilogue: With the help of community volunteers, Wanda finished the house. She vowed to get out of construction, but discovered no job as satisfying as carpentry, and chafed at taking orders from a boss. She raised more capital and resurrected Working Women Construction. She is now a respected contractor in the same small town.

Deb moved to a bigger city where she worked for a time as a union carpenter, then as a crew boss. She is now the city's first female building inspector. Over the years, both women have mellowed, and they began to correspond in an effort to deal with what they called their "leftover garbage."

Asked today to explain the breakup of their business, they will answer: undercapitalization, lack of bidding and general business experience, too much time spent on training, poor communication, different working styles, sexism. "Our ideals were laudable," they will say, "but they didn't fit with reality."

Joyce worked on the house until Wanda could no longer pay

her. Then she convinced another small contractor to hire her. She continued to work as a carpenter, gaining new skills along the way. She now has her own remodeling business, but she still credits Deb and Wanda with helping her break into the trade. "Gaining a skill was the best thing that ever happened to me," she says. "It changed my life."

A Paycheck Away

Some might call me a company woman. I've been working for Smith and Rodgers Construction since I started the carpenters' apprenticeship three years ago, and I'll probably still work for them when I turn out as a journeywoman in a year.

They like me. I work harder than most of the men. And I like them. They treat me fair, try to keep me on. That's why I'm here on the jobsite before ground has even been broken. It's a slow period for S&R. Lots of carpenters have been laid off. But not me. They find something for me to do even when there's not a single piece of wood on the job.

I don't complain. I can use the money. Christmas is coming, and my kids, they're just like all kids nowadays. Never satisfied. Plus, I have mortgage payments to make since I scraped up a down payment on a little house. Nothing fancy, definitely a fixer-upper. But, I'm a carpenter after all. I can work on it on weekends. And the kids are pretty excited to finally live in a house we own. So when the boss tells me to show up at this vacant lot, I do. Monday morning with tools, even though I can see I won't be using them today. There is no sign of construction yet, not even the sign that will say S&R Office Complex/Industrial Park. I haven't seen the prints, but I've heard this will be a multi-million-dollar project, a block square complex that should keep me and hundreds of others working for two years anyhow, maybe three.

This is a slum neighborhood. The buildings left are mostly cheap residence hotels where drunks, seamen, and old people live. The S&R trailer has been set down on one corner of the site that also serves as a parking lot for the crew. I park my VW, then go to the back of the van where I change my shoes. I hate wearing work boots, and always wait till the last minute to put them on. I pull on two pairs of wool socks, then the steel-toed boots, lacing them up tight. I take one last swig of coffee from the cup I've brought from home, then haul my toolbox out of the back, hoist it onto my shoulder and walk over to meet the crew boss, lunch box in my other hand.

I've been in the trade three years. Still I dread the first day on a new job. You never know who you'll be working with, how much attitude you'll get for being a woman. Could be the men will be fine. Could be they'll hate my guts from the minute I walk on and make no bones about it. Sometimes I think that's better than when they hate you and don't tell you. At least you know where you stand. Eventually, once I get to know the guys, I might be able to let down my defenses some, but the first day on a job I always come prepared to walk into their territory and I watch my back.

I throw open the trailer door, step inside and set down the heavy box. The crew boss is at one end, his thick body bent over a makeshift drafting table, studying prints. When he looks up, I'm relieved to recognize his Irish face.

"Hey, Jack. How ya doin'?"

"Good. Good." He smiles and extends a massive hand in greeting. "Good to have you on the job, Marie."

Jack's been with the company for 20 years. Still, he's maybe only in his early forties. Now he's no longer ambitious. He just looks to hang in till he can collect his union pension. I worked alongside him on a couple of jobs. He was a good carpenter, a company man, fast and efficient, decent to work with. Then he was hit by a piece of falling scaffolding. Did something to his back. He was out on workers' comp for a while then tried to work again, but I could see he was in pain. He'd stick a piece of two by four in his belt to keep his back straight. Lucky they made him a crew boss, or he would have been out of the trade. But that's what I like about S&R, they take care of the folks who are good workers.

Jack pulls on his brown denim jacket and we walk outside. A small, baby-faced boy, maybe 18, lopes towards us from the parking lot. Late, the first day on the job. My watch says it is two minutes after seven. The boy grins sheepishly, his long black lashes sweep downward. "Traffic," is all he says.

"No excuses," says Jack. "I want you here, ready to walk onto the job at seven sharp. Understand? Armando, you'll be working with Marie." The boy nods and looks at me. I nod back. "Get the wheelbarrow from around back. Better get a shovel, too," says Jack, and Armando moves.

Jack and I survey the site, which today looks like a bomb crater in the middle of the city. Soon, heavy equipment will be brought in and this piece of ground will be dug into a deep pit, carpenters will shore up its walls with timbers, piles will be driven down into its center and a concrete pad will be poured over the entire ground level. Then the building starts, but first we must remove all organic material that might decompose and destroy the integrity of the concrete.

I lead Armando down an earthen ramp into a honeycomb of crumbling brick walls, the remnants of ancient basements. A hallway connects a series of small rooms. Some lead directly into others. A slab of concrete juts out at street level overhead, but the weak winter sun shines through enough holes to light our way.

We put on work gloves and start hauling out debris. Bottles, hundreds of bottles and broken glass everywhere, old newspapers and magazines, sheets of cardboard, blankets, sleeping bags.

Clothing is piled in corners, hung over brick and concrete walls. Nearly every cubicle has a mattress.

We are clearing away people's homes.

Each time I push the loaded wheelbarrow out of the maze, I look for residents. No one hangs around, but by midmorning a couple of men are raiding the dumpster as we load it.

We have gone through half a dozen cubicles when I come upon one unlike all the others. The room borders on the street. Of its three walls, two are brick and the third is dug back into sandy earth. Clothes are not scattered around the dirt floor. Instead, they are hung neatly on hangers on a length of wire stretched from a rusty gas pipe on one wall to an exposed brick on the opposite: a pair of overalls, two shirts, a jacket. A woman's, I surmise from the smallness. I lift the clothes—hangers and all—from their line and throw them in the wheelbarrow. Armando and I each grip one end of the mattress made up with worn bedding and tilt it to carry it out. There is something underneath, and we set the mattress aside to look. Two color photos of children—a boy and a girl, with a woman around a birthday cake. I finger them for a moment, then stuff them in the pocket of my flannel shirt.

As we move toward the old building's edge—the concrete retaining wall that stretches up to the street—my eyes adjust to the dark, the air feels slightly warmer, and an unpleasant odor envelops us, not the smell of rotting things, not urine (though there is that.) It is sharp, pungent, almost inorganic, like a chemical pesticide.

I begin clearing out a far cubby hole, pulling at empty Thunderbird bottles, muddy pieces of cloth, when suddenly there is a movement, a shrinking movement in the corner. I am not afraid, but Armando jumps back and I am startled by his reaction. Only then am I alerted to some possible danger. We peer into the mass of a rumpled sleeping bag and at its end see the face of a man, possibly my age, staring back at us. His pale, expressionless face is covered with reddish sores, like a teenager's bad acne. His exposed hand grasps a bottle of cheap wine. Armando looks embarrassed, I think, at his own fear. But I suppose I can understand it. I might consider hurting someone who razed my home.

"You have to leave now," I say to the man. "They are building a building here," and I note to myself that I haven't admitted that I will be doing the building.

"I know," is all he says, and slowly gets to his feet, an angular, awkward body dressed in too large, too short trousers, a T-shirt and dirty, sockless sneakers. He takes only the bottle, and as he lurches away we stand aside.

Burros Bonding

"Let me buy you a drink, Alma. What'll you have?" Manny yelled from the other end of the bar. He had the bartender's attention. Then the talking stopped. Everyone waited for my answer.

"Bourbon up, water back," I grinned. The bartender nodded and a howl went up from the men at the bar.

"That ain't no ladies' drink," said Mario.

"And I ain't no lady." As I said this I caught a wink from Manny.

Manny got off his stool and came over—a small dark man whose thick head of hair had begun to gray. "Salud," he said, lifting his glass and handing mine over. "I never thought we'd be drinking together, Alma."

"Salud," I said. "Why not?"

"I don't know," he shrugged. "I thought you didn't want to drink with me. Remember the time I asked you to go out for a beer? You were afraid to go with me alone."

"Manny," I said, "I was never afraid to drink with you. I was probably just busy that night."

There is one day a year at the maintenance yard when lunch is not restricted to a half hour, and when drinking during work hours is overlooked by the bosses: the day of the retirement luncheon. On this day, we shed our blue coveralls and congregate in the cool, expansive basement of Dago Mary's, an Italian restaurant near the shipyard. On this day we may be required to work till 11 in the morning, but it is understood that no real work is expected from us in the afternoon. Most of us will be drinking, and machines do not mix well with alcohol.

During this year's lunch, Manny seemed especially buoyant, hopping up to offer toasts throughout the meal. At every opportunity glasses of red wine had been lifted. All were anxious to make the most of the celebration and to honor those coworkers whose service at the yard had come to an end.

Afterward, we all piled into trucks for the short drive back to the yard. I have my own ways of looking busy, covering myself, which is still necessary even with the unspoken agreement that no work is expected. This afternoon I've decided to be checking equipment as part of my maintenance program. That's my cover. I'm really hanging out with the guys.

I stroll through the auto shop, and out back I find Jimmy the Irishman, Johnnie and Manny drinking from paper cups.

"Here, let me find you a cup, Alma," says Johnnie. "Oh shit, you guys took all the cups."

"That's okay. Manny will share with me," I say, "won't you Manny."

"Sure," he says, filling his cup with vodka and orange juice and handing it back to me. I take a swig and hand it back. The Southern Pacific commuter train shoots by on the overpass just beyond the yard. I can see business people and office workers in suits reading papers. Only the engineers see us and wave.

"When you were a kid, did you ever walk along the tracks?" I ask Manny. "We used to put pennies on the tracks and wait for the trains to smash them."

"Sure, but we didn't have pennies," he says. "We used bottle caps. This was in Mexico. We used to play baseball in the dirt by the tracks with all the burros.

"They'd put hobbles on the burros, tie their hind legs together, then tie a rope around their necks. Poor things. Couldn't go no-where." He swigs from the cup.

Jimmy and Johnnie are arguing about the cost of the lunch. Johnnie says they charged us too much. Jimmy says we got what we paid for.

Manny turns back to me. "Did I ever tell you the joke about the Irishmen and the Italians playing football?" I'm shaking my head skeptically, never comfortable with ethnic jokes.

"See, the Irish and Italians had a game going when the train came by and blew its whistle. The Irish thought this meant the game was over, so they ran off the field. A half hour later, the Italians scored a touchdown. Ha ha, you get it?"

"Hey Alma," Manny gives me a meaningful look. "You don't really know me. We've been working together here a couple of years and you don't know who I am. Someday we have to have a little talk and I'll tell you."

"Sure, Manny."

The vodka bottle is empty and Jimmy jumps in the truck to make a booze run.

"You're taking a chance," says Johnnie. "Don't let the bosses catch you." Jimmy waves away the thought of bosses with a huge hand and guns the engine. Johnnie looks at us, shrugs and takes off to scout for bosses.

Here comes Mario from the auto body shop, red-faced and round. He resembles an Italian Santa Claus, blue coveralls stretching over a distended middle, a wave of graying hair advancing from his head.

"Hey, I've always meant to ask you something," he says to me. "Did you ever work with Jack Dexter? Good friend of mine. Says he knows you."

"Yeah. We had a business together. How is old Jack?"

"Fine as ever," he says. "Is that how you got into the trade?"

"I guess you could say that. I taught Jack everything he knows."

"Say, would you like a beer?" he asks.

I hesitate. "Sure, why not?"

Manny follows us around to the back of the auto body shop. Mario hands us both beers. "Excuse me a moment," he says, raising his eyebrows and looking toward the bathroom.

Manny's working up to something. He clears his throat.

"Look, just between you and me, I know it hasn't been all that easy for you working here. I hear what the guys say about you. That you got your job through affirmative action, you're not really qualified, that you're taking a job away from a man, you don't know your trade, you're afraid of heights…"

"Hey, wait a minute, who said I'm afraid of heights?"

This is what goes through my mind: first, I can't believe the guys would say these things about me, then I want to hear who said what and everything they said. Then I think I'd rather not know this stuff, I wish Manny would keep it to himself. Then I wonder if Manny's making it up.

"Wait, wait," he interrupts. "I know it's bullshit. You know why? It's been the same for me having brown skin. Only I been here 20 years. They wouldn't give me the good jobs. One guy even refused to work with me. I stuck it out. I made a living. But you can't trust 'em. That's all."

Mario barrels back into the shop. "Lady, have I ever told you how good you look in those Carhartts?" he booms.

"No." I turn to Manny, who's frowning with disgust. "But it only needs saying once."

Made in the USA
Las Vegas, NV
19 January 2022

41791340R00115